fish'n'tips

To Callum James Roger Nairn

Acknowledgements

As always, creating a great cookbook is a team effort, and I owe some big thankyous for *Fish 'n' Tips*. Firstly, to the indomitable Maxine Clark for her creativity, testing and styling. To Jenny Tweedie, my brilliant new assistant, who somehow managed to bring the manuscript together and keep the good ship *Fish 'n' Tips* on course through the hurricane of my life. And, as ever, a huge thanks to everybody at the Nick Nairn Cook School for their continued support and inspiration.

Many thanks to my agent Barbara Levy for introducing me to Cassell, and to Iain MacGregor and Anna Cheifetz for having faith, passion and above all, patience. To Auberon Hedgecoe and Geoff Borin for their fabulous design work and Geoff Langan for his stunning contemporary photography.

And lastly, thanks to all at Cassell for making me feel so much at home with my new publishers.

First published in Great Britain in 2006 by Cassell Illustrated,
a division of Octopus Publishing Group Limited
2-4 Heron Quays, London E14 4JP

Reprinted 2007 by Cassell Illustrated

A CIP catalogue record for this book is available from the British Library.

ISBN-13: 978-1-844034-39-0
ISBN-10: 1-844034-39-9

10 9 8 7 6 5 4 3 2 1

Edited by Barbara Dixon
Designed by Geoff Borin
Food styling Maxine Clark
Publishing Manager Anna Cheifetz
Art Director Auberon Hedgecoe

Printed in China

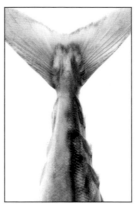

fish 'n' tips

nick nairn

CASSELL
ILLUSTRATED

Notes

Eggs: Unless otherwise stated, eggs are medium size. Try to use organic, free-range eggs.

Salad leaves: Use organic leaves.

Butter: Always use unsalted butter.

Citrus juice: Always use freshly squeezed lemon, lime or orange juice.

Frying: Use sunflower or light olive oil for shallow-frying and vegetable oil for deep-frying.

Salt: Always use sea salt, preferably Maldon.

Bay leaves: Use fresh if available. If fresh is not available, substitute with half the amount of dried bay leaves.

Contents

Introduction

For me, cooking a nice piece of fresh fish is one of life's great pleasures – almost as good as eating it. However, I do find that most people are rather wary about fish. That's possibly down to the fear of having to prepare something with eyes and scales, or perhaps it's because everyone knows someone whose granny once choked on a fish bone. I think the real problem is that, in order to sing, fish has to be fresh, fresh, fresh, and too many people have been disappointed by eating fish that's old, stale and past its best.

So that's rule number one with fish cooking: you want it spanking fresh. But since not many of us have the time, energy or resources to pop down to our local fish market at 5.00 in the morning, where do you shop?

Supermarkets, perhaps surprisingly, can supply you with a limited range of good fish and it's possible to get perfectly good salmon fillets, smoked haddock and hot water prawns from your local store. On a good day, you might even come across a decent bit of monkfish or cod.

But for really fresh fish, you have to go to a proper fishmonger. Find a shop that you can trust, and go as regularly as you can to build up a knowledge of what they have on offer. I would also encourage you to ask your fishmonger to fillet and skin the fish for you where appropriate, as it can save a lot of grief if you're not sure what you're doing.

Never shop with a completely fixed idea of what you are going to buy. If you demand a bit of John Dory, you'll be sold a bit of John Dory, even if it's on its last fins. It's a much better idea to go in with an open mind and find out what's fresh that day. A good bit of mackerel or herring fresh out the sea, although cheap as chips, will be far superior to an old bit of turbot or halibut that's been hanging around the shop for a couple of days.

You'll find that all these recipes ask for specific fish, but there's a huge amount of latitude as to what you can use. It's much more important to find the fresh fish first and adapt the recipe to what you have.

When I say fresh, I mean less than 48 hours out of the water. But unless you can completely trust your fishmonger, how do you know?

In general the main indicators of freshness are:

Bright eyes – they shouldn't be cloudy or sunken.

Firm flesh – fish tend to become soggier the longer they're out the water.

Slime – this only clings to the body for 48 hours.

Pink gills – gills oxidise and turn brown with age.

But the acid test is to use your nose. Stick your hooter in and give the fish a really good sniff. Fish shouldn't actually smell of fish. What you're looking for is a good, fresh seaside smell; think seaweed and iodine. If you smell fish at all, then it's stale.

Hopefully this should give you some good pointers, but the most important thing is not to be afraid of cooking fish. It doesn't take much effort to produce fabulous results and there's nothing better in the world than a good, home-cooked piece of fish.

round fish

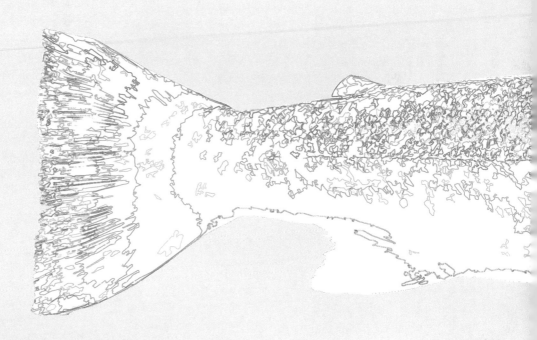

Fish pie with prawns

This is my idea of the perfect family fish pie – packed with plump prawns and big chunks of cod and smoked haddock, swathed in a creamy parsley sauce and topped with perfectly smooth, fluffy potatoes. Perfect mashed potatoes are essential here – no lumps (I press them through a ricer or a mouli for perfection). Beat the butter and milk in with an electric whisk and the potatoes will be amazingly light. This is best cooked in a big dish and brought gloriously to the table.

For the mash:

1.2kg/2½lb floury potatoes, such as
 Red Rooster or King Edwards, peeled

75g/3oz unsalted butter

250ml/9fl oz hot full cream milk

sea salt and freshly ground black pepper

For the pie:

450g/1lb fresh cod fillet, skin on

450g/1lb smoked haddock fillet, skin on

750ml/1¼ pints full cream milk

1 medium onion, peeled and
 chopped or sliced

1 fresh bay leaf

a few black peppercorns

350g/12oz cooked tiger prawns, peeled

75g/3oz unsalted butter

50g/2oz plain flour

1 tablespoon Dijon mustard

4 tablespoons (or more) chopped fresh
 flat-leaf parsley

100g/3½oz grated Cheddar cheese

Serves 6 as a main course

Preheat the oven to 180°C/350°F/gas mark 4.

Boil the potatoes in salted water for about 20 minutes until just tender. Drain and dry out in the pan over a low heat for a further 5 minutes, then mash them, beat in the butter and hot milk, taste and season. Cover them with foil and keep warm.

Meanwhile, lay the cod and smoked haddock skin-side up in a roasting tin or large wide pan. Pour in the milk and add the onion, bay leaf and a couple of peppercorns. Bring up to the boil, then reduce the heat and simmer for 5–7 minutes until just opaque. Lift out of the milk onto a plate. Strain and reserve the milk. When the fish is cool enough to handle, pull off the skin and flake the fish into large pieces, removing any bones as you go. Transfer to a large bowl and mix in the prawns.

To make the sauce, melt the butter in a medium pan. Stir in the flour and cook for 5 minutes until golden brown and biscuity, then whisk in the reserved fishy milk. Bring to the boil, then reduce the heat and simmer gently for 5 minutes until thickened. Taste and season with salt and pepper, then stir in the mustard and parsley.

Pour the sauce over the fish and give the mix a gentle stir to coat the fish with the sauce, then tip it into a pie dish. Spoon the mash on top in big dollops, then swirl together with a fork. Sprinkle on the Cheddar.

Bake in the oven for 30–40 minutes, or until the potato is golden brown and crispy. Serve immediately.

tip

It is better to under- than over-cook the fish at the first stage, so that it remains moist in the oven.

Roast cod with hummus

I've always loved hummus, and the home-made version is just light years away from the bought stuff and contains much less salt. Make a great batch of it, as it freezes well (but you have to give it a good stir once it defrosts). For speed, I make it from canned chickpeas, draining them well and rinsing under cold water to remove excess salt. The secret here is to get the balance of lemon and garlic just right. It should be very lemony and just have a hint of garlic. Make it thicker and dilute to taste.

4 cod fillets, each weighing
  150–175g/5–6oz, skinned

25g/1oz unsalted butter, plus extra
  for greasing

freshly squeezed juice of ½ lemon

150–175g/5–6oz rocket leaves

1 teaspoon sweet paprika

sea salt and freshly ground black pepper

For the hummus dressing:

125g/4oz dried chickpeas or 400g/14oz can
  chickpeas, rinsed and drained

a pinch of bicarbonate of soda

2 garlic cloves, peeled and crushed

1 teaspoon ground cumin

freshly squeezed juice of 1½ lemons

100ml/3½fl oz tahini paste
  (sesame seed paste)

6 tablespoons olive oil

3 tablespoons chopped fresh flat-leaf parsley

**Serves 6–8 as a starter,
or 4 as a main course**

If using dried chickpeas, soak them overnight in plenty of cold water. Drain, then pour them into a large pan of cold water and add a pinch of bicarbonate of soda to keep the skins soft. Bring to the boil and boil for about 45–60 minutes (test after 30 minutes) – they should be very soft. Drain well.

Put the chickpeas into a food processor with the garlic, cumin and juice of 1 lemon and blitz until sort of minced up. Add the tahini and the olive oil and blitz again until smooth. Add a little water or lemon juice to make it really creamy and sauce-like. Taste and season with salt and pepper and extra lemon juice if you think it needs it. Pour into a saucepan, beat in the chopped parsley and set aside.

Preheat the oven to 220°C/425°F/gas mark 7. Place the cod fillets on a well-buttered baking dish. Season with a little salt and pepper, dot the top of the cod with pinch-sized pieces of butter and squeeze over the lemon juice. Pour in 2 tablespoons of water, to prevent the butter from burning. Put the cod into the oven for 6 minutes, until it is just cooked (the fillets should look opaque, not cracked).

Remove the cod from the oven and allow it to rest for 2 minutes. Meanwhile, warm through the hummus and finely shred the rocket leaves.

Divide the rocket leaves between 4 warmed plates. Place the cod on top and spoon over some hummus dressing. Mix the paprika into the pan juices and drizzle over the cod. Serve immediately. This is great with just about any potato dish; in fact, I've served it with gnocchi very successfully.

Baked cod with skirlie mash, spinach and fish cream

Skirlie is a traditional Scottish dish, rather like a poor-man's haggis, but cooked in a pan instead of in a skin. It's fabulous for soaking up flavours and adds a great texture to the potatoes. The secret of success for the mash lies in the quality and type of potatoes used; a good floury variety like Red Rooster or King Edwards is essential. Older spuds work better than new and make sure that they are thoroughly cooked, but not soggy. Cod is landed all around the Scottish coast, but since North Sea cod stocks are very depleted I try and only buy cod caught in the Atlantic. This dish highlights cod's star qualities – large translucent flakes of firm-textured flesh. If you can't get cod, substitute hake or ling, or even pollack.

1 quantity Fish Cream (see page 185)

4 cod fillets, each weighing
   150–175g/5–6oz, skinned

25g/1oz unsalted butter, plus extra for
   greasing

1 tablespoon lemon juice

2 tablespoons olive oil

250g/9oz young, tender spinach leaves

sea salt and freshly ground black pepper

For the mash:

700g/1½lb floury potatoes, peeled and
   quartered

3 tablespoons milk or cream

For the skirlie:

25g/1oz good dripping or bacon fat or
   50g/2oz very finely chopped streaky bacon

½ medium onion, peeled and finely chopped

1 small garlic clove, peeled and crushed

25g/1oz medium oatmeal

25g/1oz pinhead oatmeal

1 teaspoon chopped fresh thyme

1–2 tablespoons chopped fresh flat-leaf
   parsley

Serves 4 as a main course

tips

If you like a brown crust on the cod,
quickly pan-fry it on one side only,
don't turn it, and finish it in the oven for
4–5 minutes. Serve with the browned
crust uppermost.

For the health-conscious, you can
substitute olive oil for the dripping,
but it won't have the taste.

To posh this up, add 2 tablespoons of
avruga caviar (see page 44) to the fish
cream just before serving, and dust with
chopped chives.

Preheat the oven to 230°C/450°F/gas mark 8.

Make the mash. Boil the potatoes in salted water for about
20 minutes until just tender. Drain and dry out in the pan over a low
heat for a further 5 minutes, then mash them. Add the milk or cream
and seasoning and beat everything in with a wooden spoon until nice
and fluffy. (You don't need any butter because the skirlie will add
enough fat for flavour.) Cover with foil or clingfilm and keep warm.

Make the fish cream and keep it warm.

To make the skirlie, melt the dripping or bacon fat in a heavy-based
frying pan over a medium heat. (If using chopped bacon, stir-fry over
a low heat until the fat begins to run.) Add the onion and garlic and
cook carefully for 6–8 minutes until golden, taking care not to let the
onion burn.

Increase the heat slightly and stir in both the oatmeals. Mix well until
the fat is absorbed, then turn down the heat and stir-fry for about
8 minutes until it is toasted and crumbly. Remove from the heat and
season, then stir in the thyme and parsley. Cover with foil and set
aside – don't mix with the potato yet or it will go soggy.

Heat a large saucepan ready for the spinach.

Place the cod fillets in a well-buttered baking dish. Season with
a little salt and pepper, dot the top of the cod with pinch-sized
pieces of butter and spoon over half the lemon juice. Pour in
2 tablespoons of water, to prevent the butter from burning. Put the
cod into the oven for 6 minutes, until it is just cooked (the fillets
should look opaque, not cracked).

While the cod is cooking, pour the olive oil into the preheated pan,
add the spinach and stir-fry until slightly wilted. Season it with a
little salt, pepper and the rest of the lemon juice.

Remove the cod from the oven and allow it to rest for 2 minutes.

Reheat the mash and stir in the skirlie.

To serve, lay out 4 warmed serving plates and divide the spinach
equally between them. Place a dollop of mash on top, flattening it
slightly. Place a cod fillet on top of each one and spoon over the
fish cream. Serve immediately.

Pan-fried tusk with peas and morel cream sauce

You will see tusk occasionally at the fishmonger. It swims about on its own and is usually caught by accident in amongst shoal-loving fish. It is similar to ling and both can be cooked in exactly the same way as cod. Morels are those funny brown mushrooms with the pitted, almost honeycombed caps, gathered fresh in the spring. (You can buy dried wild mushrooms, including morels in supermarkets now.) When wild mushrooms are plentiful, I make this dish a lot, whether with morels or chanterelles or whatever I can find. Fish, cream and mushrooms are a classic combination and I like to add peas for a splash of colour and sweetness.

75g/3oz dried morels

1 quantity Fish Cream (see page 185)

50g/2oz unsalted butter

4 tusk fillets, each weighing
   150–175g/5–6oz, skinned

125g/4 oz peas

sea salt and freshly ground black pepper

chopped fresh flat-leaf parsley, to garnish

Serves 4 as a main course

Soak the dried morels in 300ml/10fl oz of warm water for at least 30 minutes.

Make the fish cream and set aside while you clean the mushrooms.

Take the mushrooms out of the soaking water (reserving the liquid) and rinse them well under cold running water – a lot of grit can collect in the indentations. Squeeze them and pat dry on kitchen paper, then halve or slice any that are very big. To get rid of any grit, strain the soaking liquid through a coffee filter.

Heat the butter in a sauté pan until foaming. Add the tusk fillets. Cook without turning for 4–5 minutes. Carefully turn them over and cook for 1 minute. Transfer to a plate to rest for 2 minutes.

Add the morels to the pan and sauté for 1 minute, then add the soaking liquid and reduce by half. Now add the peas to the pan and boil fast to reduce and cook the peas. When nearly dry, add the fish cream and warm through. Taste and season with salt and pepper.

Lay the tusk fillets on warmed serving plates, spoon over the sauce and garnish with parsley. This is good with mash or a baked potato.

Baked ling with mussels, chilli and black bean sauce

Ling is the biggest of the cod family; it has a good meaty texture like cod and it steams or bakes very well. This dish is fresh and fragrant with the flavours of the ginger, spring onions and soy all doing their thing together. Make sure you use light sesame oil, and if you want, you could sprinkle over some toasted sesame seeds at the end. It's good served with noodles.

450g/1lb ling fillets, skinned and cubed

6 spring onions, trimmed

1 tablespoon groundnut or sunflower oil

2 teaspoons light sesame oil, plus extra for serving

1 garlic clove, peeled and very finely chopped

1cm/½ inch piece of fresh root ginger, peeled and finely chopped

2 tablespoons chilli and black bean sauce

2 tablespoons rice wine vinegar mixed with 2 teaspoons caster sugar

1 tablespoon dark soy sauce

900g/2lb fresh, live mussels in the shell, washed and cleaned (see page 96)

2 tablespoons roughly chopped fresh coriander

cooked medium Chinese noodles, to serve

Serves 4 as a main course

Preheat the oven to 220°C/425°F/gas mark 7. Arrange the cubed ling in a shallow baking dish.

Cut the green tops off each spring onion, slice them into long, fine shreds and set aside in a bowl of iced water. Thinly slice the remaining white parts.

Heat the groundnut or sunflower oil and the 2 teaspoons of sesame oil in a large pan. Add the white parts of the spring onions, the garlic and ginger and stir-fry for 2–3 minutes. Add the chilli and black bean sauce, rice wine vinegar dressing and the soy sauce and stir to mix.

Pour this over the ling and cover with kitchen foil. Bake in the oven for 6 minutes, then remove, add the mussels, re-cover and slam back in the oven for 5 minutes, or until the mussels have all opened. Discard any that remain closed.

Scatter with the chopped coriander and most of the drained, shredded green tops of the spring onions. Serve on a bed of cooked noodles in shallow bowls drizzled with a little more sesame oil.

Roast hake with garlic-roasted squash and crispy salami

Hake is similar to cod, though its superior flavour and softer texture warrant further attention. It is landed all around Scotland but, sadly, most of it is exported to continental Europe, where it is a prized delicacy and not just 'for your cat', as I have seen in some fishmongers.

1 large butternut squash, halved and deseeded

olive oil

6 unpeeled garlic cloves

2 tablespoons chopped fresh thyme

4 hake fillets, each weighing 150–175g/5–6oz, skinned

40g/1½oz unsalted butter, plus extra for greasing

freshly squeezed lemon juice, to taste

12 thin slices of salami

sea salt and freshly ground black pepper

Serves 4 as a main course

Preheat the oven to 200°C/400°F/gas mark 6.

First roast the squash. Cut the squash halves into quarters, arrange the pieces on a lightly oiled baking tray with the garlic and bake for 25–30 minutes until tender. Remove from the oven, scoop the flesh into a bowl and squeeze the garlic cloves into the bowl as well. Roughly mash with a fork. Stir in 3 tablespoons of olive oil and the thyme. Taste and season with salt and pepper, then keep it warm.

Turn the oven up to 230°C/450°F/gas mark 8.

Place the hake fillets in a well-buttered baking dish. Season with a little salt and pepper, dot the top of the cod with pinch-sized pieces of butter and squeeze over the lemon juice. Pour in 2 tablespoons of water, to prevent the butter from burning.

Arrange the salami on another baking sheet and drizzle with olive oil. Put both the hake and salami into the oven. Cook the hake for 6 minutes, until it is just cooked (the fillets should look opaque, not cracked). Remove the hake from the oven and allow to rest for 2 minutes. Cook the salami until it crisps up, then remove from the oven.

To serve, place a spoonful of mashed squash in the centre of 4 warmed plates. Top with the hake and pile the crisp salami on top. Drizzle around some top-notch olive oil and serve. It's delicious with a rocket salad dressed with oil and lemon juice and perhaps some grated Parmesan.

My fish and chips

The ultimate classic fish dish; so simple and yet so easy to get wrong. The important thing with chips is to choose the right variety of potato. Floury potatoes have a higher water content than waxy ones, so the flesh 'collapses' when cooked, creating a rough surface that crisps up well when fried, while the inside becomes white and fluffy. I like to use Golden Wonder, Red Duke of York or Kerr's Pink.

vegetable oil for deep-frying

900g/2lb floury potatoes, peeled

4 x 175g/6oz thick cod (haddock, ling or tusk) fillets, skinned

sea salt and freshly ground black pepper

lemon wedges and tartare sauce (see below), to serve

For the batter:

225g/8oz self-raising flour, plus extra to coat

300ml/10fl oz chilled lager

Serves 4 as a main course

Home-made tartare sauce

150ml/5fl oz Basic Mayonnaise (see page 187)

1 tablespoon chopped gherkins

1 tablespoon capers, chopped

3 spring onions, trimmed and chopped

1 tablespoon chopped fresh flat-leaf parsley or chervil

sea salt and freshly ground black pepper

freshly squeezed lemon juice, to taste

Mix the first five ingredients and season with salt, pepper and lemon juice to taste.

tips

Don't overcrowd the pan. This can cause the oil to bubble over and the temperature to drop rapidly, resulting in soggy, oily chips.

Never use an open chip pan. It doesn't do a very good job and is extremely unsafe. You can, however, use a wok (see Tip page 157)

Heat the oil in an electric deep-fat fryer to 160°C/325°F and heat the oven to the lowest setting.

While the oil is heating, cut the potatoes into chips roughly 5 x 1cm/ 2 x ½ inches and plonk into a bowl of cold water until ready for cooking (no longer than 10 minutes).

Now get all your frying equipment together. Line a colander with several layers of kitchen paper and have a slotted spoon handy. Drain the chips and rinse them. Tip them onto a clean tea towel and carefully pat them dry. Return them to the dry colander, then tip half the chips into the basket of the fryer – too many will stick together. Fry for 7–8 minutes until soft but on no account coloured. Lift out of the oil and drain on kitchen paper. Allow the oil to come back to temperature, fry the remaining chips, drain and set aside.

When almost ready to serve, reheat the oil to 180°C/350°F (190°C/ 375°F for really puffy, souffléd chips) and fry the chips in two batches for a couple of minutes until light golden brown and crisp. Drain the chips on kitchen paper and sprinkle with a little salt. Do not cover the chips or they will lose their crispness – if keeping them warm, spread them on a baking tray lined with kitchen paper in a warm oven, leaving the door slightly open (stick a wooden spoon in the door to keep it open) to let any steam escape and keep them crisp.

Now prepare the cod and batter.

Season the cod with salt and pepper and dip in the flour to coat, shaking off the excess. To make the batter, gradually whisk the flour into the lager with a good pinch of salt until you have a smooth, thick batter – don't worry, it will puff up into a light coating in the fryer.

Line a roasting tin with a good wad of crumpled kitchen paper. Dip the cod in the batter and fry for about 5 minutes until golden brown, then lift out onto the kitchen paper to absorb any excess oil.

Get the chips out of the oven as soon as the fish is cooked and serve with the crispy battered fish, plus lemon wedges and home-made tartare sauce.

Omelette Arnold Bennett
with crispy pancetta

This recipe is adapted from the original Savoy hotel recipe, which had hollandaise sauce enriching the béchamel. Lovely though that would be, I think we can do without it. Apart from being an English novelist, playwright, essayist, critic and journalist, Arnold Bennett was also a bon viveur and a director of The Savoy. This dish keeps his spirit and name alive.

Try to use real undyed, cold-smoked Finnan haddock fillets rather than the glow-in-the-dark dyed variety (goodness only knows what they use to dye it).

225g/8oz undyed smoked Finnan
   haddock fillets

300ml/10fl oz full cream milk

50g/2oz unsalted butter

25g/1oz plain flour

100g/3½oz Cheddar or Gruyère cheese,
   or a mix of the two, grated

1 teaspoon Dijon mustard

a dash of Worcestershire sauce

8 thin rashers of pancetta

6–8 eggs

2 tablespoons freshly grated
   Parmesan cheese

freshly ground black pepper

Serves 4 as a lunch main course

tip

When poaching haddock, slip it into the water or milk skin-side up to prevent it drying out during cooking.

Poach the haddock in the milk for 3–5 minutes. Using a slotted spoon, lift the haddock out of the milk and set on a plate. Reserve the milk. Pick over the haddock and remove any skin and bones, then roughly flake the fish. Preheat the grill to hot.

Now make the béchamel. Melt 40g/1½oz of the butter in a small saucepan and stir in the flour to make a roux, combining until smooth. It's important at this stage to make sure the flour is cooked, so fry the roux until golden and smelling biscuity, then whisk in the reserved fishy milk. Continue to cook over the heat, whisking until the sauce is thick and smooth. Beat in the grated cheese, mustard and Worcestershire sauce, then put to one side and keep the sauce warm.

Grill the strips of pancetta until crisp, then remove and keep them warm. Leave the grill turned on.

Whisk the eggs, then season with pepper only and stir in half of the haddock.

Heat a large frying or omelette pan, add the remaining butter and swirl around the pan to coat it really well. Pour in the egg and haddock mix and cook very quickly, pulling the cooked egg into the centre of the pan and allowing the uncooked egg to run to the edges, until it is just cooked, but still a bit wet.

Scatter the remaining haddock on top and spoon over the béchamel. Sprinkle with the Parmesan and crumble over the pancetta, then brown under the hot grill.

Serve immediately, straight from the pan, with a really big fresh salad – either slide the omelette onto a large serving plate or, if you're a bit worried about getting the omelette out in one piece, cut into wedges and serve.

Smoked haddock and fusilli gratin

This is a sort of posh, fishy macaroni cheese, ideal for entertaining larger groups. I have a large gratin dish at home that can serve 12 people, and this dish just happens to work well as a double batch.

450g/1lb undyed smoked haddock fillets, unskinned

600ml/1 pint full cream milk

1 onion, peeled and finely chopped

1 fresh bay leaf

450g/1lb dried fusilli

6 rashers of rindless, smoked streaky bacon

600ml/1 pint Mornay Sauce made with the poaching milk (see page 122)

2 tablespoons chopped mixed fresh herbs, such as flat-leaf parsley, chives and thyme

350g/12oz cherry tomatoes, halved

4 tablespoons freshly grated Parmesan cheese

sea salt and freshly ground black pepper

Serves 6 as a main course

Preheat the oven to 180°C/350°F/gas mark 4.

Lay the haddock fillets skin-side uppermost in a roasting tin. Pour over the milk and add the onion and bay leaf. Cover with greaseproof paper and bake in the oven for 12–15 minutes, or until the haddock is cooked – it should be opaque and firm.

Meanwhile, bring a large saucepan of salted water to the boil, add the fusilli and cook for 10–12 minutes until al dente, then drain and set aside.

Heat a frying pan over a medium heat, add the bacon and dry-fry for 3–4 minutes until brown and crisp. Remove from the pan, drain on kitchen paper and chop roughly.

When the haddock is cooked, lift out of the milk and, when cool enough to handle, remove the skin and any bones, then flake the fish. Set aside.

Strain the milk and use to make the Mornay sauce. Add the herbs and season to taste with salt and pepper.

To finish, spoon one-third of the fusilli into an ovenproof dish, followed by half the flaked haddock, half the bacon and half the sauce. Top with a second layer of fusilli, followed by the remaining haddock and bacon. Top with the remaining fusilli and finish with the remaining sauce. Scatter the halved tomatoes over the top, sprinkle with the Parmesan and bake in the oven for 25–30 minutes until the gratin is hot and bubbling and the top is brown. Serve very hot.

tip

You can put the whole dish together up to 24 hours before you do the final cooking. Just lower the oven temperature to 160°C/325°F/gas mark 3 and increase the cooking time to 45 minutes.

Smoked haddock and spinach crêpes with Parmesan cream

Another step back in time, but like all great dishes, this one still delivers great eating, regardless of the decade. Smoked haddock, spinach and cream will never go out of fashion.

For the crêpe batter:

2 eggs

100g/3½oz plain flour

250ml/9fl oz full cream milk

about 50g/2oz Clarified Butter
  (see page 186), melted

For the haddock and spinach filling:

450g/1lb undyed smoked haddock fillets,
unskinned

600ml/1 pint full cream milk

1 onion, peeled and finely chopped

1 fresh bay leaf

500g/1lb 2oz baby spinach leaves

600ml/1 pint Mornay Sauce made with the
  poaching milk (see page 122)

freshly squeezed lemon juice, to taste

unsalted butter for greasing

2 tablespoons freshly grated Parmesan
  cheese

sea salt and freshly ground black pepper

**Serves 6 as a starter, or 4 as a
main course**

tip

The pancakes can be made in
advance and even frozen, layered
with greaseproof paper.

Preheat the oven to 180°C/350°F/gas mark 4.

To make the crêpe batter, break the eggs into a bowl. Add the flour and whisk until thick and lump-free. Now whisk in the milk and half the melted butter until smooth. The batter should have the consistency of single cream. Set aside and leave to rest for 1 hour.

Next, cook the fish. Lay the haddock fillets skin-side uppermost in a roasting tin, pour over the milk and add the onion and bay leaf. Cover with greaseproof paper and bake in the oven for 12–15 minutes, or until the haddock is cooked – it should be opaque and firm.

Meanwhile, cook the spinach in a large pan until just wilted. Remove, drain and chop. When the haddock is cooked, lift out of the milk (reserving the milk) and, when cool enough to handle, remove the skin and any bones, flake the fish and add to the spinach. Set aside.

Strain the milk and use to make the Mornay sauce. Stir one-third of the sauce into the fish and spinach and fold together, then season to taste with salt and pepper and lemon juice.

Now make the pancakes. Heat a 15–18cm/6–7 inch crêpe pan until hot. Brush with a little clarified butter, pour in some of the batter (about 2 tablespoons) and tilt the pan until the mixture covers the base in a thin, even layer. As soon as you have cooked a couple you will be able to judge how much you will need for the rest. Cook over a high heat for 1–2 minutes, until golden underneath, then lift up the edge with a palette knife, flip it over and cook for 30–60 seconds longer, until lightly browned. Tip out onto a plate. Brush the pan with a little clarified butter as necessary and continue like this, layering the crêpes up with squares of greaseproof paper, until you have made about 12.

Divide the haddock mixture between the pancakes and roll them up or fold into triangles. Arrange them in one layer in a buttered baking dish and spoon over the remaining sauce. Sprinkle the top with the Parmesan and bake in the oven for 25–30 minutes until the gratin is hot and bubbling and the top is brown. Serve very hot.

My favourite smoked haddock kedgeree

This Anglo/Indian concoction works well with any smoked haddock. But the gentle spicing, for some unknown reason, always puts me in mind of the more intense flavour of Arbroath Smokies, the Rolls Royce of the smoked haddock world.

175g/6oz basmati rice

75g/3oz unsalted butter

1 small garlic clove, peeled and finely chopped

1 bunch of spring onions, trimmed and chopped

1 large, fresh red chilli, deseeded and chopped

1 tablespoon mild curry paste

2 Arbroath Smokies (one pair), skinned and flaked, or 350g/12oz smoked haddock fillets, cooked and flaked

12 semi-dried, sun-blush or Confit Tomatoes (see below), halved

4 soft-boiled eggs

3 tablespoons chopped fresh flat-leaf parsley or coriander

freshly ground black pepper

Serves 6 as a starter,
or 4 as a main course

Confit tomatoes

12 large, ripe plum tomatoes

50ml/2fl oz decent olive oil, plus extra for preserving (approx. 200ml/7fl oz for a 600ml/1 pint preserving jar)

1 sprig of fresh basil or thyme

1 garlic clove, peeled and crushed

sea salt and freshly ground black pepper

Makes 24

Cook the rice according to the manufacturer's instructions.

Melt the butter in a large sauté pan, add the garlic, spring onions and chilli and cook for 1 minute. Stir in the curry paste to coat and a couple of grindings of pepper, then add the rice and stir well. After 4 minutes, add the haddock and tomatoes and cook until thoroughly warmed through. Tip onto a large, warm serving dish.

Peel the eggs, cut into quarters and arrange over the kedgeree. Scatter with the chopped parsley or coriander and serve while still hot.

Confit tomatoes

Preheat the oven to 110°C/225°F/gas mark ¼.

Slice the tomatoes in half, through the growing eye at the top. Then remove the green eye. Lay the tomatoes on a baking sheet cut-side up, sprinkle lightly with crushed sea salt and pepper and drizzle the 50ml/2fl oz olive oil over them.

Place the tomatoes in the oven (you may have to prop the oven door slightly open to keep the temperature down) and leave for 8 hours.

When you return, the tomatoes should be reduced to half their original size, but not browned. Turn them over and leave for a further 4 hours, or until they are nice and firm.

Remove the tomatoes from the oven and leave until cool. Then place them in a preserving jar, add the sprig of basil or thyme and the garlic and cover in olive oil. These ultra-tasty beauties can now be stored in your fridge for up to 3 weeks.

I realise that this take a fair bit of time to do, but it is worth it. The only way you'll find out is if you try ...

tips

Forego the supermarket chains and make Confit tomatoes yourself. But beware, it's important to obtain really good, ripe plum tomatoes – the little Dutch waterballs won't work.

Approximately 12 hours of oven time is involved in the making of these, so don't plan on using your oven for anything else that day. Better still, you can do them overnight. It's worth it – they are a taste sensation.

Smoked haddock croquettes with sweet and sour beetroot

There is something of the school dinner at play here, but trust me, the contrast between the crunchy, smoky croquettes and the sweet, sour and earthy beetroot is a winner.

750g/1lb 10oz floury main crop potatoes, such as King Edwards or Maris Piper

25g/1oz unsalted butter

900g/2lb Arbroath Smokies

1–2 tablespoons double cream

25g/1oz seasoned plain flour

1 egg, beaten

75g/3oz fresh white breadcrumbs

vegetable oil for deep-frying

sea salt and freshly ground black pepper

For the sweet and sour beetroot:

3 medium-sized raw beetroots

4 tablespoons white wine vinegar

2 tablespoons light soft brown sugar

2 shallots, peeled and finely chopped

2 tablespoons chopped fresh chives

Serves 6 as a starter

tips

The croquettes can be frozen once breaded. Just defrost them overnight in the fridge on some kitchen paper.

Make the sweet and sour beetroot up to 3 days ahead.

For the croquettes, peel the potatoes and cut them into chunks. Cook in boiling, salted water until tender. Drain well, then tip back into the pan and mash with the butter until smooth. Press through a sieve with a wooden spoon or use a mouli to make a very smooth purée, and leave to cool a little.

Meanwhile, skin and bone the Arbroath Smokies and break the flesh into small pieces. You should be left with about 350g/12oz of flaked fish. Add the flaked fish, cream and a little salt and pepper to the potatoes and mix well. Divide the mixture into 12 and roll into barrel shapes. Place on a baking tray, cover with clingfilm and chill for 20 minutes.

For the sweet and sour beetroot, put on some rubber gloves to avoid staining your hands, then peel the beetroot and grate into a bowl. Add all the remaining ingredients except the chives and place in a medium pan with 4 tablespoons of water. Bring to the boil, then reduce the heat and simmer for 15–20 minutes until thickening and most of the liquid has evaporated. If it's still a bit runny, increase the heat and cook for a couple more minutes, stirring well. Remove from the heat and allow to cool. Once cold, stir in the chives, season with salt and pepper, cover and chill until needed.

Heat the oil in a deep-fat fryer to 180°C/350°F. Dip the croquettes into the seasoned flour, then the egg and then the breadcrumbs, pressing the breadcrumbs on well to give a thick, even coating. Cook the croquettes, four at a time, for about 4 minutes until crisp and golden. Lift each batch out onto some kitchen paper and keep them warm in a low oven (150°C/300°F/gas mark 2) while you cook the rest.

Bring the beetroot to room temperature. Place 2 croquettes on each plate, pile the sweet and sour beetroot alongside and serve while the croquettes are still hot and crunchy.

My favourite soused herring

One of my favourite starters, soused herrings are herrings 'cooked' in vinegar. It's a bit like ceviche – the acid in the vinegar cures or cooks the fish. The vinegar is balanced by the addition of sugar to give a sweet/sour flavour and it pickles the cucumber inside the herring. This method of pickling suits oily fish like herring down to the ground, and if you can't get herring you could use mackerel. I love the fiery kick of wasabi and am usually quite generous with the hot, green paste. But you may not want to overdo it. You can make this in big batches and keep the fish in sterilized airtight Kilner jars in the fridge, but only if you use very fresh herring and good-quality vinegar with a 5% acidity. It will improve with time and keeps for up to one month.

6 fat herring fillets

50g/2oz fine sea salt

½ cucumber, peeled and halved lengthways

1 sheet of nori seaweed (optional, it's there for the flavour)

wasabi paste, to taste

1 red onion, peeled and very finely sliced

For the marinade:

600ml/1 pint rice wine vinegar or good-quality white wine vinegar

4 tablespoons caster sugar

1 star anise

12 whole peppercorns

Makes 6 as a starter

Lay the herring flesh-side up in a shallow dish and sprinkle liberally with the salt. Cover and leave for 2–3 hours to draw out the water.

Make the marinade. Put the vinegar in a pan with the sugar, star anise and peppercorns and slowly bring to the boil. Once boiling, take off the heat and leave to cool.

Scoop the seeds out of the cucumber and cut the cucumber into matchsticks. Divide into 6 small bundles. Cut the nori seaweed (if using) into 6 strips and wrap each of the bundles with a strip of nori.

Remove the herring from the salty liquid, rinse in cold water and pat dry on kitchen paper. Spread each herring with a tiny amount of wasabi paste. Wrap a herring around each nori bundle and secure closed with a cocktail stick.

Place a layer of onion over the base of a dish that will take the herring in a single layer. Arrange the herring closely together on top of the onion and pour over the cooled vinegar, making sure the fish are covered. Cover and refrigerate for at least 4 days before eating. (Alternatively, stack the rollmops into a preserving jar and pour over the vinegar in the traditional way. Just make sure they are covered by the liquid.)

Serve the drained rollmops with a little of the pickled onion, some crusty bread and a green salad.

Mackerel tagine

Moroccans cook most fish with a spicy marinade called chermoulah. It varies from region to region and some are quite hot with plenty of chilli powder. As the fish in this dish takes little time to cook, the vegetables are cooked first in a rich tomato sauce, then the fish is laid on top to steam and roast. Carrots are a great favourite and their sweetness goes very well with the oiliness of the fish.

3 large mackerel, filleted

1 quantity Chermoulah (see Barbecued sardines with chermoulah, page 37)

3 large floury potatoes, peeled and cut into 1.5cm/¾ inch square chunks

3 carrots, peeled and cut into 1.5cm/¾ inch chunks

3 ripe plum tomatoes, chopped, or 12 cherry tomatoes

12 Confit Tomatoes (see page 26), or shop-bought

2 garlic cloves, peeled and and finely chopped

1½ tablespoons tomato purée

4 tablespoons freshly squeezed lemon juice

6 tablespoons sunflower oil

150ml/5fl oz water

sea salt

chopped fresh coriander, to garnish

Serves 6 as a main course

Lightly rub the mackerel fillets with salt and let stand for 10 minutes (this will firm them up and intensify their flavour). Rinse and pat dry. Lay them in a shallow dish and rub all over with half the chermoulah, then cover and marinate for at least 30 minutes.

Preheat the oven to 200°C/400°F/gas mark 6.

Toss the potatoes and carrots in half the remaining chermoulah and lay them in the bottom of a shallow casserole. Scatter with both types of tomatoes and sprinkle with the garlic.

Mix the remaining chermoulah with the tomato purée, lemon juice, oil and water. Pour this sauce over the vegetables. Cover tightly with kitchen foil and a heavy lid and bake for 35 minutes until the vegetables are tender.

Remove the lid and lay the fish fillets skin-side up over the vegetables. Baste with the juices, then bake uncovered for 15–20 minutes, or until the fish is cooked, the juices thick and concentrated and the vegetables beginning to brown.

Serve warm, not hot, scattered with chopped coriander. This is great with couscous flavoured with the juice and zest of a lemon and fresh mint.

tip

If you don't feel like filleting the fish, you can cook them whole, but remember to slash through the flesh on both sides before marinating.

Grilled sardines on toast (bruschetta) with salsa verde

This knocks the spots off mashed, canned sardines on soggy, white toast. Salsa verde is a clean, sharp-tasting sauce from Italy that I find works best with oily fish like sardines. I like to use sea-salted capers rather than the vinegared sort as they taste much better – but they must be rinsed well to get rid of the salt. Italians say the best capers are the tiny ones from the island of Pantelleria, off the coast of Sicily, but since they're a little hard to get hold of, the ones from the supermarket will do just fine. The sauce is at its best used on the day of making, but will keep for 2–3 days in the fridge.

4 thick slices good-quality sourdough bread

4 tablespoons olive oil

1 garlic clove, peeled and halved

8–12 fresh whole sardines, depending on size, scaled, cleaned and boned (see page 11)

50g/2oz seasoned plain flour

sea salt and freshly ground black pepper

lemon wedges, to serve

For the salsa verde:

2 garlic cloves, peeled

4 anchovy fillets in oil, drained, rinsed and chopped

3 tablespoons each chopped fresh flat-leaf parsley, mint and basil

1–2 tablespoons sea-salted capers, rinsed and chopped

75ml/3fl oz good-quality extra virgin olive oil

2 tablespoons freshly squeezed lemon juice

Serves 4 as a starter

tip

To protect your chopping board from the garlic smell, place a sheet of greaseproof paper over it before you chop the garlic.

First make the salsa verde. Using the flat edge of a chef's knife, crush the garlic with a pinch of sea salt until it breaks down into a cream. Stir in the remaining ingredients and season with pepper. Or, if you don't want to be fussy, you can just toss all the ingredients into a food processor and pulse briefly until combined – do not over-process. If not serving immediately, transfer to a jar and pour a layer of olive oil on top to exclude the air.

Heat a griddle pan to medium heat. Brush the bread slices with half the oil and place on the griddle for 1–2 minutes on each side until nice and crisp. A word of warning, keep an eye on the temperature – if it's too hot you'll end up with scorched bread before it has a chance to crisp up. (If you don't have a griddle pan, simply bake the bread on a baking sheet in a medium oven, 180°C/350°F/gas mark 4, for 4–5 minutes.) When the bread is done, rub the cut clove of garlic over the surface of each slice and keep them warm.

Preheat the grill to hot. Dip the sardines in the seasoned flour and shake off the excess. Lay them skin-side up on a grill pan and drizzle with the remaining oil. Cook under the hot grill for 1–2 minutes (don't turn them) until golden and cooked through. (Alternatively, heat a frying pan to medium heat and add 1 tablespoon of oil. Fry the sardines for about 1 minute on each side until they are golden and just cooked through.)

Spread the bruschetta with salsa verde, top each one with two or three sardines and serve with extra salsa verde and lemon wedges.

Oriental tartare of salmon

This dish relies on the acid in the lemon juice to do the cooking, and I've encountered numerous versions over the years. This one takes its flavouring from sashimi and partners well with the pickled cucumber. Use sushi-quality salmon for this dish.

½ cucumber, about 200g/7oz

freshly squeezed juice of 1 large lemon

1 tablespoon light sesame oil

1 tablespoon sunflower oil

1 teaspoon wasabi powder mixed with water
to a thick paste

1 tablespoon Japanese soy sauce
(Kikkoman's)

2 tablespoons finely chopped Japanese
pickled ginger

450g/1lb salmon fillet, skinned and very
finely chopped

sea salt and freshly ground black pepper

1 sheet of nori, finely shredded, to garnish
(optional)

Serves 4 as a starter

Peel the cucumber and thinly slice lengthways on a mandoline. Whisk salt and pepper into half the lemon juice, then whisk in the sesame oil. Toss the cucumber slices in the mixture and leave to marinate for about 1 hour.

Whisk the remaining lemon juice, the sunflower oil, wasabi, soy sauce and chopped ginger together. Add salt and pepper to taste and toss with the salmon.

To serve, pack a quarter of the mixture into a chef's ring on each plate. Remove the ring and pile a quarter of the cucumber on top. Garnish with shredded nori (if using). Do not keep them for more than 30 minutes before serving, or they will over-cure.

tip

As an alternative, you can use half salmon
and half tuna.

Smoked salmon with apple salad and wasabi dressing

I love the combination of salty smoked salmon, crunchy sweet apple and punchy wasabi. At my Cook School we use our own smoked salmon – which is particularly good – but go for the best that you can find.

4 tablespoons light olive or sunflower oil

2–3 tablespoons freshly squeezed lemon juice

½ teaspoon wasabi powder

½ tablespoon mayonnaise

2 eating apples, cored and grated

300g/10oz smoked salmon, thinly sliced

175g/6oz mixed crunchy leaves, such as romaine, iceberg, cos, etc.

sea salt and freshly ground black pepper

Serves 4 as a starter

In a medium bowl, whisk the oil, lemon juice and wasabi powder together. Taste and, if necessary, adjust the seasoning.

Pour half of this dressing into a larger bowl and whisk the mayonnaise into the remaining dressing. Mix the grated apple and smoked salmon into the mayonnaise dressing and toss well to coat. Taste and season.

Toss the salad leaves in the larger bowl with the plain wasabi dressing.

Serve a pile of salad leaves topped with a dollop of dressed apple and smoked salmon mix.

tip

Powdered wasabi keeps for longer and is better than the unnatural luminous green stuff in tubes.

Smoked salmon, oatmeal blinis and horseradish cream

These blinis originate from Russia and are traditionally served with smoked salmon and caviar. They are yeasted pancakes, lightened with whisked egg white. I use oatmeal for a Scottish twist, but they are traditionally made with buckwheat flour. The combination of crème fraîche and horseradish works with smoked salmon beautifully. The avruga is perhaps gilding the lily, but it looks good and adds a luxurious note.

a handful of young salad leaves
about 450g/1lb thinly sliced smoked salmon
4 teaspoons avruga caviar (see page 44)
fresh chervil or dill, to garnish

For the blinis:
65g/2½oz fine oatmeal
75g/3oz plain flour
a pinch of fine sea salt
2 teaspoons caster sugar
175ml/6fl oz warm full cream milk
15g/½oz fresh yeast
2 egg whites
2 tablespoons chopped fresh flat-leaf parsley
olive oil for frying

For the horseradish cream:
50g/2oz good-quality crème fraîche
50g/2oz good-quality mayonnaise
20g/¾oz fresh horseradish, finely grated
freshly squeezed lemon juice, to taste
sea salt and freshly ground black pepper
chopped chives, to garnish

Serves 4 as a starter

To make the blinis, mix the oatmeal, flour and salt in a large bowl. Add the sugar to the warm milk and crumble in the yeast, mixing thoroughly. Pour the milk mixture into the flour and oatmeal and gently stir together. When well mixed, cover with clingfilm and leave in a warm place until the mixture rises and doubles in size.

For the horseradish cream, place the crème fraîche and mayonnaise in a bowl and mix in the horseradish. Add the chives and season to taste with salt, pepper and lemon juice. Cover and chill.

Back to the blinis. Whisk the egg whites to a soft peak, then fold a spoonful into the risen batter to loosen the mixture. Fold in the rest of the egg whites and add the parsley.

Heat a small blini pan and add a splash of olive oil. Add a ladle of blini batter and cook for 3–4 minutes over a medium heat or until the mixture is golden on the base. Flip over and repeat until the colour is the same on both sides. Cook the remaining blinis in the same way, then stack together, wrap loosely in foil and keep warm.

To serve, place the warm blinis on 4 warmed plates and place a spoonful of horseradish cream on top. Top this with salad leaves, then carefully place 4 thin slices of smoked salmon on top of each one. Add a twist of black pepper and a teaspoon of avruga. Garnish with chervil or dill and serve immediately.

Whole poached sea trout with sorrel sauce

Poaching fish whole is the only way to go for good cold fish, as the skin and bones both flavour the flesh and keep it moist. This recipe also tastes great when warm, but is just a bit fiddly come serving time so you might find fillets are easier. Both sorrel and sea trout are at their prime at the same time of year – early summer.

1.5–1.8kg/3½–4lb whole sea trout, cleaned and trimmed

1 recipe Court Bouillon (see page 182)

1 quantity Butter Sauce (see page 186)

100g/3½oz fresh sorrel leaves, tough stalks removed, roughly chopped

Serves 4 as a main course

tips

If using fillets instead of a whole fish, strain the court bouillon into a wide pan, just deep enough to cover the sea trout. Bring up to barely simmering and slip in the fillets. Poach for 5–7 minutes until opaque and just set. Serve whilst still warm.

Your fishmonger may sometimes hire out fish kettles – it's worth asking.

To poach the sea trout, use a large fish kettle and lay the cleaned fish on the perforated rack. Pour in the court bouillon and make sure the fish is completely covered with the liquid. Bring slowly up to the simmer, then poach for 15–18 minutes, until the flesh is opaque to the bone when tested with the point of a knife. (For cold sea trout, turn off the heat once simmering, and leave to cool in the liquid – this will keep it very moist for serving cold.)

Meanwhile, make the butter sauce and keep it warm.

To serve the sea trout hot, lift it out of the fish kettle, rack and all. Drain well and, using 2 sturdy fish slices and steady hands, carefully lift on to a serving platter.

Quickly stir the sorrel into the butter sauce and pour into a warm sauceboat or bowl. Carry the fish to the table and serve with the sauce. Don't let this sauce hang around – the sorrel loses its colour quickly once heated.

To serve the fish, take a sharp knife and cut through the skin along the length of the back and around the gills. Lift away the skin, then turn the fish over and remove the skin from the other side. Now run the knife along the line marking the 2 fillets and ease them apart and away from the bones. Lift the fish off the bone onto warmed plates, lifting the backbone away to reveal the lower fillets. You only need to add some boiled buttery new potatoes to complete the perfect summer meal.

Baked sea trout with courgette fritters and tomato and orange vinaigrette

Baking sea trout is perhaps the easiest way to cook them.

4 x 150g/5oz sea trout steaks or fillets

25g/1oz unsalted butter

3 tablespoons white wine

a little freshly squeezed lemon juice

sea salt and freshly ground black pepper

For the tomato and orange vinaigrette:

150g/5oz very ripe cherry tomatoes, halved

2 tablespoons olive oil

finely grated zest and juice of ½ orange

For the courgette fritters:

3 medium courgettes, coarsely grated

1 teaspoon sea salt

2 eggs, separated

75g/3oz plain flour

150ml/5fl oz double cream

2 spring onions, trimmed and finely chopped

sunflower oil for frying

Serves 4 as a main course

If preparing in advance, place the steaks or fillets on a baking tray, dot with butter and pour round 2–3 tablespoons of white wine, water or stock. Cover with clingfilm and store in the fridge until ready to cook.

To make the tomato and orange vinaigrette, place the tomatoes in a liquidiser with the olive oil, orange zest and juice. Give it a quick blitz to break down the tomatoes (it'll take about 45 seconds), then empty the liquid into a fine sieve. (Alternatively, use a hand blender.) Push it through with a ladle, taste for seasoning and keep to one side until ready to serve.

For the courgette fritters, mix the grated courgettes with the salt and leave to drain in a sieve for 15 minutes. Rinse off the salt, squeeze out the excess water and dry well on kitchen paper.

Whisk the egg yolks and flour together in a bowl and then whisk in the cream to make a smooth batter. Stir in the spring onions and the courgettes.

When ready to cook, preheat the oven to 220°C/425°F/gas mark 7.

Whisk the egg whites together in a separate bowl until they form soft peaks – make sure they don't get too stiff or they won't fold into the rest of the mixture. Fold a large spoonful of whites into the courgette mixture to loosen it slightly, then gently fold in the remainder.

Pour about 1cm/½ inch of oil into a large frying pan or wok. Using half the mixture, drop in 2 large spoonfuls of the batter, keeping them separate, and fry for 3–4 minutes on each side over a medium heat until golden. Drain on kitchen paper and place on warmed plates, or under a low grill, while you cook the other two and then cook the sea trout.

Season the trout with salt, pepper and lemon juice and bung them into the oven for 5–6 minutes until opaque and just cooked. Warm through the tomato and orange vinaigrette, but don't boil.

Place a courgette fritter in the centre of each warmed plate and rest a piece of sea trout on top. Spoon a little of the tomato and orange vinaigrette around the edge of each plate and serve.

Pan-fried sea trout with courgette relish

Pan-frying sea trout properly produces a wonderfully tasty, golden crust on the outside, whilst the interior remains yielding and moist. Make sure the frying pan is at the correct temperature: too cold and the fish won't colour; too hot and it will burn; get it right and you will hear a nice sizzle as the raw fillet hits the pan. Leave the fish alone to allow the all-important crust to form, don't fiddle with it.

4 sea trout fillets, skin on, each weighing about 150g/5oz

sunflower oil

15g/½oz unsalted butter

sea salt and freshly ground black pepper

For the courgette relish:

175g/6oz onions, peeled and sliced

1 garlic clove, peeled and crushed

2 tablespoons olive oil, plus extra for frying the courgettes

25g/1oz soft light brown sugar

1 teaspoon tomato purée

50ml/2fl oz balsamic vinegar

1 tablespoon Worcestershire sauce

2 ripe plum tomatoes, halved, deseeded and diced

450g/1lb courgettes, cut into 1cm/½ inch dice

Serves 4 as a main course

To make the relish, sweat the onions and garlic in the olive oil for 5 minutes, until softened but not coloured. Add the sugar, tomato purée, vinegar, Worcestershire sauce and diced tomato and simmer for 20 minutes until very thick, then remove from the heat.

Now sauté the courgettes in small batches over a very high heat, using about 1 tablespoon of olive oil per batch, for about 1 minute until lightly browned. This is very important – if you cook too many courgettes at a time over too low a heat they will release their liquid, which will make the chutney go runny. Season, then stir them into the tomato and onion mixture. Cover and leave for at least 2–3 hours to allow the flavours to soften and infuse. When ready to serve, gently warm the relish over a low heat and keep it warm.

Heat a frying pan over a high heat. Add a little sunflower oil, then add the sea trout fillets skin-side down and sear for about 2 minutes (without moving) until the skin is crisp and golden. Turn them over, add the butter and cook the other side for about 2 minutes, then season with a little salt and pepper. Remove the fish from the pan onto a plate and leave to stand and relax for 2–3 minutes before serving.

To serve, place a pile of the relish in the centre of each plate, then place the sea trout on top of the relish.

tips

Frying the fish on the skin side really crisps the skin up and keeps the flesh beautifully moist.

The relish benefits from being made in advance and will keep for up to 10 days in the fridge.

Sea bass en papillote with marjoram and lemon

I love cooking fish in foil or parchment parcels as all the flavour and moisture is locked in. They're also great for preparing in advance and bunging in the oven at the last minute. Cooking the fish over the veg means that all the fish juices are absorbed into the dish and not lost. Use nice, big, wild sea bass fillets for this rather than the smaller, farmed ones.

4 x 150g/5oz sea bass fillets, skinned

olive oil for brushing

1 carrot, peeled and finely shredded

2 celery sticks, finely shredded

4 spring onions, trimmed and finely shredded

2 tablespoons chopped fresh marjoram

8 thin slices of lemon

a little dry white wine or freshly squeezed lemon juice

sea salt and freshly ground black pepper

Serves 4 as a main course

Preheat the oven to 190°C/375°F/gas mark 5.

Cut 4 large rectangles of baking parchment big enough to wrap each fish fillet generously. Brush each piece of parchment with a little oil and lay them out on a work surface.

Season the fillets with salt and pepper. Mix the vegetables together in a bowl and season with salt and pepper. Divide the vegetables between the parchment sheets, keeping them to one side of each rectangle of paper to make a bed for the bass fillets. Lay one fillet on top of each pile of vegetables and sprinkle with the marjoram. Lay 2 slices of lemon over each fillet and sprinkle with the wine or lemon juice.

Loosely fold the free half of the parchment over the fish and twist or fold the edges tightly together to seal. Lay the packets on a baking tray and bake in the oven for 15 minutes.

Serve immediately on warmed plates, allowing everyone to open their packages at the table.

tip

This is great served with some little new spuds tossed in butter.

Pan-fried sea bass with chilli soy greens

Sea bass probably has the best flavour of any white-fleshed fish. Get your fishmonger to scale and fillet it for you. Farmed Greek sea bass is now widely available, and perfect for this dish. Save the more expensive and superior line-caught fresh bass for simple grilling, some melted butter and a wedge of lemon. Pak choy (bok choi) is available from most large supermarkets and is a bit like a chunky lettuce with a white fleshy stem. It only needs a minimum of cooking and that has to be done at the last minute. You'll need both a frying pan and a wok (or two large frying pans). You'll also need shallow bowls to serve this in as the veg is quite soupy.

4 small sea bass fillets, skin on

275g/10oz pak choy, each quartered

2 tablespoons sunflower oil

1–2 fresh red chillies, deseeded and
  finely diced

about 1 tablespoon Thai fish sauce
  (nam pla)

finely grated zest and juice of 1 lime

2 tablespoons Japanese soy sauce
  (Kikkoman's)

4 tablespoons black bean sauce

250ml/9fl oz hot Marinated Vegetable Stock
  (see page 184)

2 tablespoons chopped fresh coriander

freshly squeezed lemon juice, to taste

sea salt and freshly ground black pepper

Serves 4 as a starter

Season the bass fillets with salt, pepper and lemon juice. Cook the pak choy and the bass simultaneously, so heat two frying pans (or one frying pan and a wok for the greens) and add 1 tablespoon of oil to each.

Put the bass fillets skin-side down in one pan and the bok choy and chillies in the other. Stir-fry the leaves and chilli until wilted, then stir in the fish sauce, 1 teaspoon of the lime juice, the lime zest, soy sauce and black bean sauce. Add the hot stock and chopped coriander and bring to the boil, then taste and add more lime juice if necessary. You may also need to add more fish sauce. Keep warm.

Turn the fish fillets after 3–4 minutes. The skin should be crisp. Cook the other side for 1 minute only, then lift the fish out of the pan and season with a little salt and pepper.

To serve, heap a mound of pak choy in the centre of each of 4 shallow bowls and spoon the sauce around. The bass fillets go on top and you're ready to go.

tips

If this all sounds a bit frenetic, the bok choy can be cooked first and kept warm in a bowl.

Two 450g/1lb fish will give 4 starter-sized portions.

For a main course, double up the fish and serve it with some basmati rice or noodles.

Peppered tuna steaks

Look out for top-quality tuna for this dish – it should have a firm, meaty texture and be dark, glossy and dry, just like a good steak. For this reason, I like to give it a steak-like treatment. I've used a mixture of green and black peppercorns here, but you can use just the black kind if you prefer.

1½ tablespoons black peppercorns

1½ tablespoons dried green peppercorns

2 tablespoons sunflower oil

4 thick tuna steaks, each weighing about 150g/5oz

4 teaspoons Dijon mustard

50g/2oz unsalted butter

1 tablespoon freshly squeezed lemon juice, or to taste

sea salt

Serves 4 as a main course

Crush the peppercorns coarsely in a coffee grinder or pound in a pestle and mortar. Tip the pepper into a fine sieve and shake out all the powder. This is very important because the powder will make the tuna steaks far too spicy. Now spread the peppercorns over a small plate. Smear both sides of the tuna steaks with the mustard and coat them in the crushed peppercorns. Only now season with salt, because salting first would prevent the pepper sticking to the fish. Set aside.

Heat a large frying pan until hot. Add the oil and then the tuna steaks and give them a couple of minutes on either side (a bit longer if you don't like your fish rare, but do not overcook them). Do not move them around once they are in the pan or the peppercorn crust will fall off – the aim is to produce a good crusty coating on each surface.

Now add the butter to the pan and allow it to colour to nut brown, basting the tuna steaks with the buttery juices as you go.

Squeeze over the lemon juice and serve each steak with the buttery juices poured over the top and a huge green salad on the side. You'll find it is very rich. Chips or sautéed potatoes would also be appropriate.

tips

Always buy thick tuna steaks – thinner ones cook too quickly and tend to become too dry.

Don't overcook tuna, it should always be pink in the middle.

Tuna, salmon and halibut sashimi

There's nothing quite like the sea-fresh taste of sashimi tempered with the bite of stinging wasabi and the cool crunchiness of fresh white mooli. Only make this when you can get hold of some spanking fresh fish, as the freshness of the fish is all-important for sashimi. Some fishmongers will pre-cut fish for sashimi, but the best result comes from slicing it yourself at the last moment straight out of the fridge whilst it is still firm. Some people are surprised that sashimi is quite chunky rather than being wafer thin, but this is necessary to get the correct mouth-feel whilst eating it.

5cm/2 inch length mooli, peeled

150g/5oz piece of best tuna fillet, taken from the thin end of the loin

150g/5oz piece of best salmon fillet, skinned

1 thick halibut fillet, skinned

wasabi paste made from powder, to taste

4 tablespoons Japanese pickled ginger, drained (reserve the juice) and shredded

Japanese soy sauce (Kikkoman's), to serve

Serves 4 as a starter

Finely shred the mooli on a mandoline, then plunge into iced water for about 30 minutes to crisp it up. Drain and pat dry with kitchen paper.

Slice each piece of tuna, salmon and halibut across the grain at a 45-degree angle. Each piece of fish should give you 8 slices about 5mm/¼ inch wide. Hold the slices together to retain the shape of the piece of fish.

To serve, put a mound of mooli and a tiny mound of wasabi paste on each plate. Add 1 tablespoon of shredded pickled ginger to each plate as well. Arrange 2 slices of each fish sitting vertically on the plates and serve with a small dish of Japanese soy sauce. I like to add some of the drained juice from the ginger to the soy sauce for extra pep.

Tuna with white bean and rosemary purée

Antony Worrall Thompson cooked this bean and rosemary purée during a visit to the Cook School, but served it with chargrilled chicken. By chance, he was also demonstrating a tuna dish and I tried some tuna with the bean purée. Bingo! A marriage made in heaven. So here's my version.

4 thick tuna steaks, each weighing about 150g/5oz

sea salt and freshly ground black pepper, to taste

olive oil, to serve

For the bean purée:

250ml/9fl oz extra virgin olive oil, plus extra oil for drizzling

4 garlic cloves, peeled and lightly crushed

2 sprigs of fresh rosemary, stripped from the stalk

2 large dried red chillies, crushed

2 x 400g/14oz cans cannellini beans, rinsed and drained

about 450ml/15fl oz chicken stock

1 large bunch of flat-leaf parsley, stalks removed, coarsely chopped

8 spring onions, trimmed and finely sliced

1 teaspoon very finely chopped fresh rosemary

freshly squeezed juice of ½ lemon

Serves 4 as a main course

To make the bean purée, pour the oil into a saucepan, add the garlic, rosemary and chillies and cook over a low heat until the garlic and chillies colour and are golden. Strain the oil and discard the rosemary, chillies and garlic. Keep the oil warm.

Meanwhile, heat the beans in the chicken stock. You may not need all the stock, just enough to cover the beans. Cook until the beans are heated through, but don't boil. Drain the beans, retaining the liquor.

Place half the beans and 150ml/5fl oz of the chicken stock in a food processor and blend until smooth. With the machine still running, add the warm oil in a thin trickle until the purée is shiny and has the consistency of a thickish mayonnaise.

Using a rubber spatula or spoonula, scrape the purée into a bowl, add the remaining beans and lightly crush with a fork. Now add the remaining ingredients and mix well. Season to taste and keep the purée warm. This can be made ahead of time and reheated with a little stock. If making in advance, smear the surface with olive oil to prevent a skin from forming. Cool, cover with clingfilm and refrigerate. Warm through to serve.

Meanwhile, heat a ridged grill pan until very hot. Season the tuna steaks and place them 2 at a time on the pan. Cook for 2 minutes, then turn each steak at a 90-degree angle (but still cooking on the same side) and cook for a further 2 minutes. Turn the steaks over and repeat the process, but be careful not to over-cook the tuna. If the steaks are thin, you may need to cook them on one side only (serve with the crosshatched markings uppermost).

Keep the first 2 steaks warm while you cook the second batch in a similar fashion, then serve straight away with a dollop of the white bean purée and a drizzle of good olive oil.

tip

Add a spoonful of tapénade (see page 64) to the purée.

Tuna teriyaki with noodle salad

Real Japanese teriyaki sauce is used as a basting sauce rather than a marinade, but personally, I'm greedy and want a double hit of the delicious teriyaki flavour, so I do both. Japanese mirin, or saké, has the unique ability to coax out and accentuate the natural flavours of foods. Mirin's mild sweetness balances the salty soy sauce and is used to enhance sweet as well as savoury sauces. It is particularly good with fish. Foods in teriyaki are usually seared and then basted with the sauce throughout cooking – this stops the outside burning to a crisp, and produces a delicious, glossy glaze.

4 tuna loin steaks, each about 1.5cm/¾ inch thick

groundnut or sunflower oil for basting

For the teriyaki sauce:

1 small garlic clove, peeled and finely chopped

1 teaspoon freshly grated root ginger

2 tablespoons caster sugar

150ml/5fl oz Japanese soy sauce (Kikkoman's)

150ml/5fl oz mirin, saké or dry sherry

For the noodle salad:

1 teaspoon light sesame oil

1 tablespoon sunflower oil

finely grated zest and juice of ½ lime

2 fresh green chillies, deseeded and shredded

1 teaspoon fresh ginger juice (pressed through a garlic press)

1 head of pak choi, shredded

small bunch of fresh coriander, roughly chopped

50g/2oz raw peanuts, chopped

100g/3½oz dried medium egg noodles, cooked and dressed with sunflower oil

sea salt and freshly ground black pepper

Serves 4 as a main course

Put all the ingredients for the teriyaki sauce into a shallow dish and mix until well blended. Add the tuna steaks and turn to coat all over. Cover and refrigerate for at least 30 minutes – or even overnight.

When ready to cook, light the barbie or heat the grill.

Meanwhile, make the noodle salad. Whisk the sesame oil with the sunflower oil, lime zest and juice, chillies and ginger juice to make the dressing. Add the shredded pak choi, coriander and the peanuts to the cooked noodles and pour in the dressing. Toss well and season to taste.

Remove the tuna from the marinade and pat dry with kitchen paper. Keep the marinade for basting.

Brush both sides of the tuna with oil, then cook over hot coals (or in a foil-lined grill pan under a very hot grill) for about 2 minutes on each side, basting several times, until dark and glossy on the outside but still pink on the inside. Serve immediately with the noodle salad.

tips

The thickness, not the weight, of the tuna is important for the cooking time to be correct, especially when barbecuing.

Tuna is best cooked rare, as it can be dry and dense if over-cooked.

Spice-crusted, seared carpaccio of tuna

This is a great dish to experiment with if you're a first-timer in the raw fish department as there is a little layer of cooked meat on the outer edge to disguise the raw texture. Just remember to slice it very thinly. Use sashimi-grade tuna and make sure it is super fresh. You might be lucky enough to find it in a supermarket, but your best bet will be a decent fishmonger.

2 tablespoons sunflower oil

225g/8oz loin of tuna taken from a large fish, well trimmed

2 tablespoons Sichuan peppercorns

½ teaspoon sea salt

1 teaspoon Chinese five-spice powder

For the marinade:

2 tablespoons dark soy sauce

2 tablespoons sunflower oil

1 tablespoon runny honey

finely grated zest and juice of 1 lime

2 teaspoons fresh ginger juice (pressed through a garlic press)

To garnish:

sprigs of fresh coriander

pickled ginger, shredded

lime wedges

Serves 6 as a main course

Mix all the ingredients for the marinade and pour into a shallow dish.

Heat a large frying pan until it is very hot, add the oil, then sear the tuna over a high heat, turning it now and then, until it has cooked all over to a depth of about 5mm/¼ inch. Transfer the tuna to the marinade, turning it occasionally as it cools, and leave until cold.

Meanwhile, heat a dry, heavy-based frying pan over a high heat. Add the peppercorns and toss for a few seconds until they darken slightly and start to smell aromatic. Tip them into a mortar and coarsely crush them with the pestle. Stir in the salt and five-spice powder, then sprinkle the mixture onto a plate. Lift the tuna out of the marinade (reserving the marinade) and dip it in the spices so that they form a thin, even coating. Wrap the fish tightly in clingfilm and chill for 24 hours.

To serve, remove the tuna from the fridge and unwrap it. Using a long, very sharp knife, slice the loin across into very thin slices. Lay three or four slices on each plate and garnish with the coriander, pickled ginger and a wedge of lime. Serve the marinade separately as a dipping sauce.

Red mullet grilled with tapénade and sauce vierge

This is a really quick dish, and a fitting use for some fab fresh red mullet. It's delicious served with couscous, and is particularly good with home-made pasta because of the mix of delicate textures. Sauce vierge is just a posh name for virgin olive oil sauce, essentially good-quality olive oil infused with Mediterranean flavours. Ripe tomatoes are essential – my current favourites are the small vine tomatoes or cherry plum tomatoes (pomodorini).

4 x 100g/3½oz red mullet fillets, unskinned
olive oil for brushing

For the sauce vierge:
120ml/4fl oz decent olive oil
2 shallots, peeled and finely chopped or
    sliced
1 garlic clove, peeled and lightly crushed
    but still whole
4 ripe plum tomatoes, roughly chopped
    (or the equivalent in cherry tomatoes)
2 tablespoons roughly chopped fresh basil
freshly squeezed juice of ½ lemon
sea salt and freshly ground black pepper

For the tapénade:
2 garlic cloves, peeled and finely chopped
100g/3½oz anchovy fillets in oil, drained
100g/3½oz sea-salted capers, rinsed and
    drained
100g/3½oz pitted black olives (the crinkly
    ones), weighed after pitting
3 tablespoons extra virgin olive oil
freshly squeezed lemon juice, to taste
olive oil for sealing

Serves 4 as a starter

To make the Sauce Vierge, place the oil, shallots and garlic in a small pan and warm through on a gentle heat until the sauce is hot, but not boiling – you want to soften those shallots, not colour them. Heat this way for 10 minutes, then remove from the heat and set aside. (The sauce can be made to this point several days in advance and kept in the fridge.)

Now make the tapénade. Put the garlic, anchovy fillets, capers and olives in a food processor and blitz until the mix forms a coarse paste. Then add the olive oil and blitz again. Add lemon juice to taste and scrape out into a jar, smooth down the surface and cover with a thin layer of olive oil. You will have more than enough for this recipe. This will keep in the fridge for at least 10 days.

When ready to cook the fish, preheat the grill to its hottest setting.

Using a very sharp knife, lightly slash the mullet diagonally on the skin side. Gently spread the tapénade over the slashed sides. Line a grill pan with foil and brush it with olive oil. Lay the fillets on the foil and drizzle with extra olive oil. Grill for about 3 minutes, or until cooked through and opaque. Remove from the grill and keep the fish warm while you finish the sauce.

Remove and discard the garlic clove from the sauce, then stir in the tomatoes, basil and lemon juice. Return to the heat to warm through and season with salt and pepper. Serve with the grilled mullet.

tips

If the red mullet are very small, grill them whole after slashing the sides and spreading with tapénade.

Red mullet is a very delicate fish, treat it with care.

Red mullet escabèche

In Spain, escabèches were originally created to preserve fish, and it is still a very popular way of preparing fish, especially in tapas bars. If you can't find red mullet, use small sea bass or mackerel. Ask your fishmonger to fillet the mullet for you as it is quite tricky. Check for any tiny, stray bones.

8 x 100g/3½oz red mullet fillets, unskinned
plain flour for dusting
2 tablespoons olive oil
sea salt and freshly ground black pepper

For the marinade:

175ml/6fl oz decent olive oil
1 large carrot, peeled and thinly sliced
1 medium onion, peeled and finely sliced
4 garlic cloves, peeled and thinly sliced
1 small fresh red chilli, deseeded and thinly
  sliced (optional)
200ml/7fl oz red wine vinegar
200ml/7fl oz dry white wine
200ml/7fl oz Fish Stock (see page 181)
a long strip of orange peel
2 fresh bay leaves
2 sprigs of fresh thyme
2 sprigs of fresh rosemary
6 whole peppercorns

Serves 8 as a starter

First, make the marinade. Heat 75ml/3fl oz of the oil in a medium saucepan and add the carrot, onion, garlic and chilli. Cook for 5–8 minutes until soft and just beginning to colour. Add another 75ml/3fl oz of oil, the vinegar, wine, fish stock, orange peel, bay leaves, thyme, rosemary and peppercorns. Bring to the boil and boil fast for 2–3 minutes to reduce the liquid and cook out the raw vinegar flavour. Set aside while you cook the fish.

Season the fillets and dip in the flour, shaking off the excess. Heat a heavy frying pan until medium-hot. Add the 2 tablespoons of oil, then place the fillets in the pan, skin-side down, and cook for 1½ minutes on each side, until just cooked through and golden.

Carefully lift the fish out of the pan and lay them in a shallow dish, skin-side up. Pour over the marinade, cool, cover and refrigerate for up to 12 hours. Bring to room temperature before serving.

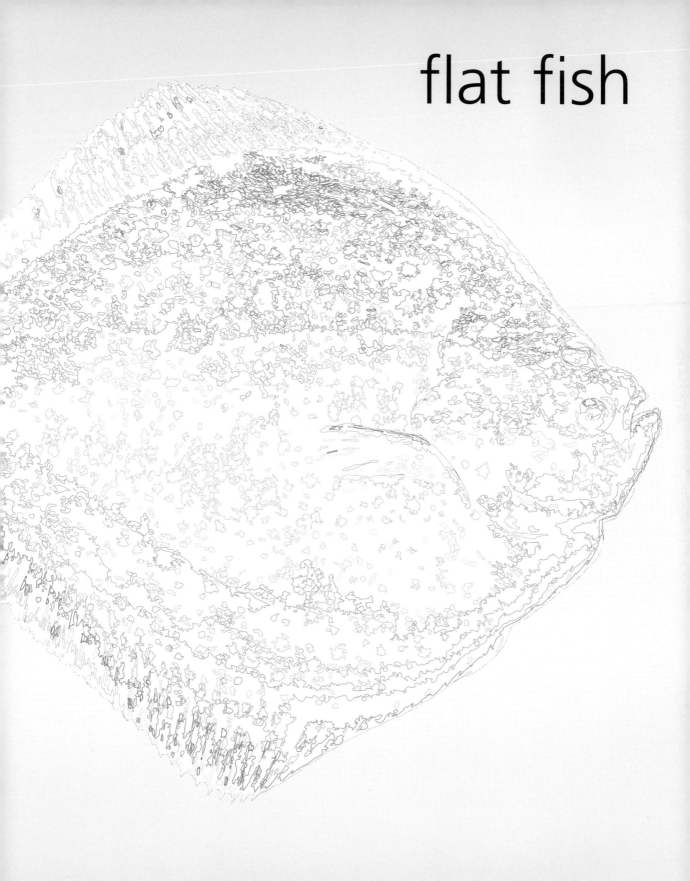

flat fish

Cooking flat fish

Despite the fact that they're never going to win any beauty contests, flat fish produce the most prized, and therefore most expensive, flesh in the fish world. Their rather sedentary lifestyles result in rich, meaty fillets and a peculiar anatomy means that the fillets are also bone-free. It's nature's way of saying 'eat me'!

Turbot

Turbot is probably my favourite white fish and it's at its best cooked simply on the bone, as in the Baked Turbot on the Bone with Lemon and Shrimp Cream (see page 83), although it's also very good pan-fried. The slightly gelatinous flesh of the turbot really helps to prevent it from drying out too much during cooking. You'll find that it's reassuringly expensive and you should look for a sizable specimen (the bigger the better!) with fillets or steaks cut from fish up to about 6kg/13lb in weight.

Sole

Dover sole is a superb fish and a real treat when you can find it. The best size is around 300–500g/11oz–1lb 2oz and, like turbot, it's best cooked on the bone. Simple dishes such as Classic Grilled Dover Sole and Sole à la Meunière (see pages 74 and 77) help to accentuate its subtle flavour. In your average fish-mongers, you're more likely to come across lemon sole fillets and these are absolutely fine for most dishes. You should also look out for the less common Megrim or Witch sole, both of which are meaty and delicious.

Halibut

Halibut tends to be the biggest of the flatfish and gives good, meaty fillets. It's lower in fat than turbot and needs careful cooking to avoid drying out. I tend to bake or pan-fry it.

Skate

A relation of the shark, skate is delicious, but only the wings are edible and the fresher the better. I think skate is best poached, but you can also pan-fry it.

John Dory

Although not a proper flat fish, as it has eyes on either side of its head, John Dory has a highly compressed body and lurks close to the sea bed. When shopping for fillets, look for big ones cut from fish weighing 1.5kg/3½lb or bigger if you can get them. Pan-fried, these are a personal favourite of mine.

Monkfish

A big ugly fish in a class of its own, whole monkfish are easily recognisable due to their huge heads and gaping mouths, but it's usually just the tails that are sold. These provide two long fillets on either side of a soft bone, though you'll find the fillets covered by a membrane, which should be removed before cooking. Monkfish has a unique meaty texture and fine sweet flavour, and the fillets are best pan-fried, roasted or baked.

Steamed roulade of skate
with tapénade and ratatouille

We used to serve this at my Glasgow restaurant, Nairns – and very popular it was, too. It's ideal for a posh dinner party, as everything can be prepared in advance, just leaving the final steaming to the end. The Mediterranean flavours of ratatouille and tapénade really complement the delicate flavour of the skate.

1 tablespoon olive oil

4 large skate wings, trimmed and skinned (ask your fishmonger to do this)

1 quantity of Tapénade: (see page 64)

sea salt and freshly ground black pepper

sprigs of chervil, to garnish

For the ratatouille:

2 small red peppers, roasted, skinned, deseeded and cut into 5mm/¼ inch dice

2 plum tomatoes, skinned

1 sprig of thyme

600ml/1 pint hot Marinated Vegetable Stock (see page 184)

1 small yellow pepper, roasted, skinned, deseeded and cut into 5mm/¼ inch dice

1 small aubergine, trimmed and cut into 5mm/¼ inch dice

1 medium courgette, cut into 5mm/¼ inch dice

Serves 4 as a main course

To make the ratatouille, add half the diced red peppers, all the tomatoes and the thyme to the hot stock, then simmer, uncovered, for 20 minutes. After simmering, blitz with a hand blender or liquidise thoroughly. Strain through a fine muslin cloth set in a sieve over a jug to catch the juice. Put the resulting juice in a saucepan and add the remaining red peppers, the yellow peppers and the aubergine. Simmer for 6–8 minutes, then add the courgette and cook for 3 minutes. Check the seasoning, then set aside.

Heat the oil in a large heavy-based frying pan until hot. Season the skate wings with salt and pepper and then seal in the hot pan for 2 minutes on each side. You will probably have to cook the wings in batches. Leave the skate to cool, then remove the meat from the bones. It should be underdone at this stage.

Lay a large piece of clingfilm (about 30cm/12 inches square) on a work surface and lay the skate meat out over the clingfilm in an even layer, all the strands of fish pointing away from you. Using a palette knife, carefully spread a thin layer of tapénade evenly across the fish. Using the clingfilm, roll the fish as tightly and evenly as you can away from you – in the same way that you would do for a Swiss roll. Once rolled, tie the clingfilm at each end, roll the whole thing in a fresh layer of clingfilm and then refrigerate for at least 4 hours to firm up.

Using a sharp knife, cut the roulade into four 7cm/3 inch slices and place them in a steamer for 4–5 minutes until just cooked through.

Heat the ratatouille through.

Remove the skate from the steamer and take off the clingfilm. Place each piece in the centre of a large warmed bowl. Spoon the ratatouille broth around the roulade and garnish with some sprigs of chervil.

Poached skate with brown butter and capers

Poaching skate keeps this delicate and under-rated fish incredibly moist. The French call this browned butter beurre noisette, the colour of hazelnuts – that is, cooked until the buttermilk in the butter caramelises to a nutty brown colour, but does not burn. Always ask your fishmonger to skin the skate for you – it is a nasty business to do at home, and remember, overcooked skate is lost! Serve with boiled potatoes and wilted greens.

1.2 litres/2 pints Court Bouillon (see page 182)

4 skate wings or pieces, total weight 900g–1.35kg/2lb–2¾lb

100g/3½oz unsalted butter

1 tablespoon white wine vinegar or lemon juice

2 tablespoons sea-salted capers, rinsed

2–3 tablespoons chopped fresh flat-leaf parsley

sea salt and freshly ground black pepper

Serves 4 as a main course

Pour the court bouillon into a wide shallow pan and add the skate in a single layer. Cover and bring slowly to the boil. Just before the water boils, reduce the heat and cook at a bare simmer – the water should hardly move – for 8–10 minutes until cooked through (do not overcook – skate should be very moist).

Meanwhile, melt the butter in a small saucepan over a medium heat and continue to cook until it turns a shade lighter than deep brown (watch out as this can burn quickly). Snatch off the heat and pour in the vinegar or lemon juice, swiftly followed by the capers and parsley. Stir well and return to the heat to warm through, but don't let it boil or the butter will burn.

Carefully lift the skate out of the pan, drain well and place on 4 warmed plates. Spoon over the browned caper butter, season with salt and pepper and serve immediately.

tips

If skate smells of ammonia it should be rejected.

Generally one skate wing of 225–300g/ 8–11oz is one portion. Large skate wings can be cut in half vertically to give two good portions.

Goujons of sole and real tartare sauce

This recipe is for real fish fingers or 'goujons', as they say in France. White fish fillets cooked this way are totally irresistible – we served them at my three-year-old daughter's birthday party and they were a big hit with adults and kids alike. They combine brilliantly with tartare sauce – basically mayonnaise with lots of nice green things like gherkins, capers and parsley stirred in. For convenience, I often use a good-quality, shop-bought mayonnaise, but avoid the low-fat variety. The sole fillets should be chunky and really fresh or they won't taste of anything. Cut across the grain diagonally to help them hold together, and please use natural dried breadcrumbs, not that horrible dyed orange stuff called fish dressing.

450g/1lb thick sole fillets, skinned

4 tablespoons seasoned plain flour

2 eggs, beaten

100g/3½oz natural dried breadcrumbs

vegetable oil for deep-frying

sea salt and freshly ground black pepper

lemon wedges, to serve

For the tartare sauce:

150ml/5fl oz Basic Mayonnaise (see page 187) or shop-bought

2 tablespoons chopped gherkins

2 tablespoons chopped capers (for this recipe the ones in vinegar will do)

2–3 tablespoons finely chopped fresh flat-leaf parsley

1 shallot, peeled and finely chopped

finely grated zest and juice of 1 lemon, to taste

a couple of drops of Tabasco

Serves 4 as a starter

tips

Freeze the crumbed goujons and cook from frozen (increase the cooking time to about 6 minutes).

You can make the breadcrumbs up to 12 hours in advance.

To prepare the goujons, cut the sole fillets across the grain diagonally into thick 'fingers'.

Have 3 dishes ready, one with seasoned flour, one with beaten egg and the third with breadcrumbs. Toss the fingers in the flour and shake off the excess. Next, dip the sole fingers in batches into the beaten egg, turning them around until well coated. Give them a bit of a shake and dunk them in the breadcrumbs, tossing them about until they are evenly coated. At this stage you can lay them on a tray (as long as they don't touch), cover them with clingfilm and refrigerate for up to 12 hours until you are ready to cook. Or you can freeze them (see Tips below).

Before you cook the goujons, make the tartare sauce – this is best freshly made and doesn't keep well. Put the mayonnaise in a bowl and stir in the gherkins, capers, parsley and shallot. Add about 1 teaspoon lemon zest, Tabasco to taste and season with salt, pepper and extra lemon juice. Taste and adjust until it's nicely balanced. Transfer to a serving bowl and chill until you're ready to serve.

Line a large plate or tray with a wad of kitchen paper, have a slotted spoon handy and have your serving dish warming. Preheat the oven to 140°C/275°F/gas mark 1 and heat the oil in a deep-fat fryer to 190°C/375°F.

Fry the goujons a few at a time for 3–4 minutes until crisp and golden. Drain each batch on the kitchen paper and sprinkle lightly with salt. Keep them warm in the oven with the door slightly ajar (they will go soggy if closed) while you cook the rest.

Serve with the tartare sauce for dipping and dunking, and lots of juicy lemon wedges.

Classic grilled Dover sole

For me, this is the very best way to cook Dover sole. Amongst chefs, however, there is a divergence of opinion as to exactly how it is best done: all skin on, all skin off, dark skin only off. Help! Anyway, here's what I do. Ask your fishmonger to trim the frills around the edge of the fish, remove the tail, and pull off the dark skin, but leave on the white. This way, when you grill the fish skinless-side up, the thickest fillets are nearest the grill, and the white skin stops the fish sticking to the bottom of the pan.

1 Dover sole, about 400g/14oz, per person, cleaned and scaled, with dark skin removed

50g/2oz unsalted or Clarified (see page 186) butter, melted, plus extra to serve

freshly squeezed lemon juice, to taste

sea salt and freshly ground black pepper

chopped fresh flat-leaf parsley and lemon wedges, to serve

Serves 1 (or the number of sole you can comfortably fit under your grill)

Preheat the grill to its highest setting.

Pat the fish dry with kitchen paper. Lay a piece of foil in your grill pan and brush it and the skinless side of the fish with plenty of melted butter. Season with salt, pepper and lemon juice and place the fish, skin-side down, under the grill, but not too close to the heat.

Grill without turning for about 10 minutes until the fish is cooked through and opaque at the bone. Carefully lift off the white skin before serving, and serve the fish with the grill pan juices, extra melted butter, chopped parsley and lemon wedges.

tip

A flexible fish slice is a bit of a must for moving the fish.

Baked sole with prawn and ginger cream

This dish gives loads of flavour for minimum effort. The fresh zingy flavour of root ginger prevents what is quite a rich dish from becoming cloying and heavy. Be careful not to overcook the prawns – they just need to be warmed through in the ginger cream, which can be prepared ahead if you want to save time.

4 x 175g/6oz sole fillets, skinned,
   or 8 smaller ones

40g/1½oz unsalted butter, plus extra for
   greasing

freshly squeezed juice of 1 lemon

3cm/1¼ inch piece of fresh root ginger,
   peeled and cut into fine julienne
   (matchsticks)

300ml/10fl oz double cream

225g/8oz freshly cooked, peeled prawns

3 tablespoons chopped fresh coriander
   and chives

sea salt and freshly ground black pepper

Serves 4 as a main course

Preheat the oven to 190°C/375°F/gas mark 5.

Lay the sole fillets in a well-buttered baking tray. Dot with 25g/1oz of the butter, splash over some lemon juice and season well. Bake for 7–8 minutes, depending on the thickness of the fillets.

While the sole is baking, sweat the ginger in the remaining butter for 5 minutes to soften, but not colour. Pour the cream over the ginger and season well. Bring the cream to the boil, then reduce the heat and simmer for 2 minutes until slightly thickened. Stir in the prawns, a good squeeze of lemon juice and the chopped herbs. Do not allow to boil.

Carefully lift the sole off the baking tray onto four warmed plates. Pour any collected pan juices into the cream sauce and mix well. Check the seasoning, then pour over the sole, ensuring you divide the prawns equally. Serve with basmati rice and some wilted greens.

tip

If you prefer a more luxurious dish, use langoustines instead of prawns and/or use half Langoustine Stock (see page 183) and half cream, and reduce really well to thicken it.

Roast turbot with creamy lemon potatoes, fine beans and Parma ham

The potato garnish used in this dish is a variation on gratin Dauphinoise, but substitutes the lemon zest for the garlic. This produces a fabulous flavour, which partners most fish extremely well. I've upped the normal amount of cream to give it a creamier texture, so you don't need a sauce here.

1 tablespoon sunflower oil
1 tablespoon Clarified Butter (see page 186)
4 x 175g/6oz turbot fillets
freshly squeezed lemon juice, to taste
sea salt and freshly ground black pepper

For the creamy lemon potatoes:
150ml/5fl oz full cream milk
300ml/10fl oz double cream
finely grated zest of 1 lemon
2 pinches of sea salt
1kg/2¼lb potatoes, preferably Maris Piper
   or similar
25g/1oz Parmesan cheese, freshly grated
   or 50g/2oz Gruyère cheese, grated
butter for greasing

For the beans:
250g/9oz fine beans
4 slices of Parma ham

Serves 4 as a main course

tip

Use turbot steaks if you can't find fillets.

Preheat the oven to 150°C/300°F/gas mark 2.

First make the potatoes. Butter a medium ovenproof dish. Pour the milk into a large ovenproof pan (i.e. no plastic handle) and add the cream, lemon zest, salt and a good few grindings of pepper. Peel and thinly slice the potatoes on a mandolin grater (or in a food processor) – you really can't get them thin enough by hand, and even if you could, you'd die of boredom doing all this lot! Do not rinse them – you want the starch to thicken up the mix. Add the potato slices to the pan one by one to coat them evenly with the cream and milk – the slices often stick together if you just bung them all in. Bring to the boil, then reduce the heat and simmer until the potatoes are almost tender and the potato starch has thickened the milk – about 10 minutes.

Either turn the potatoes into the buttered dish, or just use the pan to oven-cook the potatoes. Sprinkle the top with the cheese (this will give the dish a golden crust). Bake in the oven for about 40 minutes until nicely browned on top. As there is extra cream in this recipe, the potatoes will be very creamy and not set. Serve immediately or leave to cool overnight. To reheat, pop into the oven at 150°C/300°F/gas mark 2 for 30 minutes.

Cook the beans in plenty of salted water for about 4 minutes, or until al dente. Drain and plunge into a bowl of iced water to stop them cooking. Drain and dry, then divide into 4 bundles and wrap each bundle in a slice of Parma ham. Place on a baking tray and reheat in the oven for 10 minutes with the potatoes.

To cook the turbot, heat the oil in a large frying pan. Add the clarified butter and the turbot fillets and fry over a high heat for 3–4 minutes on each side until just cooked through. Lift them out of the pan onto a warm plate to prevent them from cooking any further, season with salt, pepper and a little lemon juice and keep them warm while you assemble the dish.

Serve each turbot fillet with a dollop of potatoes and a bean parcel.

Turbot with cabbage, garlic and carrot with grain mustard sauce

Sweet, meaty turbot likes a bit of quality grain mustard and here it gets it in a glossy butter sauce. The carrot and cabbage combination is one of my favourite vegetable garnishes and works well in a huge range of different dishes, from fish to lamb to game. It is also a fully paid up member of the mustard fan club.

4 x 175g/6oz turbot steaks

freshly squeezed lemon juice, to taste

75g/3oz unsalted butter

2 garlic cloves, peeled and crushed

2 medium carrots, peeled and grated on
  a box grater

450g/1lb Savoy cabbage, cored and finely
  shredded

1 quantity Butter Sauce (see page 186)

1–2 tablespoons best-quality grain mustard

sea salt and freshly ground black pepper

Serves 4 as a main course

Season the turbot steaks with salt, pepper and lemon juice. Heat a heavy-based frying pan until hot, add half the butter and, when foaming, lay the turbot steaks into the pan. Fry over a medium heat for about 4 minutes, then carefully turn them over and cook for a further 4 minutes. Transfer to a warm plate to rest while you cook the cabbage.

Add 4 tablespoons of water to the same unwashed frying pan and add the rest of the butter. Bring to the boil, scraping any fishy bits that have stuck to the bottom of the pan. Add the garlic and boil for 1 minute. Now add the carrot and cabbage and cook for 3–4 minutes, tossing and stirring over a high heat until lightly coloured and most of the juices have evaporated.

Reheat the butter sauce and stir in the mustard to taste.

Serve the turbot steaks on a bed of garlicky cabbage with the mustard sauce spooned over.

tip

For extra flavour and luxury, add 75g/3oz of shredded, good-quality smoked salmon to the cabbage. Mix it in 2 minutes from the end, and lose the garlic.

Turbot baked on the bone with shrimp cream

Turbot tastes best when baked whole like this. The fish retains more of the flavour if cooked on the bone, and the gelatinous skin keeps it moist. The cooked fillets can be easily lifted off the skeletal frame if you know what you are about – you just need a thin filleting or fish knife and a little knowledge of fish anatomy. This used to be an art practised by waiters in posh restaurants right in front of the diner. These days, sadly, you don't see it being done too often.

50g/2oz unsalted butter
1.5kg/3½lb whole turbot, cleaned and gutted
freshly squeezed juice of 1 lemon
sea salt and freshly ground black pepper

For the shrimp cream:
300ml/10fl oz double cream
100g/3½oz peeled brown shrimps
2 tablespoons chopped fresh chives

Serves 4 as a main course

Preheat the oven to 180°C/350°F/gas mark 4.

Take a large roasting tin that is big enough to accommodate the turbot and grease it generously with some of the butter.

Using a big sturdy knife or a cleaver and scissors, cut the head off the fish. Lay the turbot in the tin and dot the top of it with the rest of the butter. Pour over the lemon juice and season the fish with some salt and pepper. Slide the tray into the oven and leave it to roast, uncovered, for 30 minutes. Remove the turbot from the oven, cover and leave to rest for 5 minutes.

Meanwhile, make the shrimp cream. Bring the cream to the boil in a medium pan, stir in any collected pan juices from the turbot and boil briskly for 2 minutes. Now stir in the shrimps and chives and warm through, but be careful not to boil. Check the seasoning, but it shouldn't need any.

To serve, run a knife down the backbone of the fish and transfer the top 2 fillets to warmed serving plates. Lift off the bone and then put the remaining 2 fillets on the other two plates.

Serve with boiled new potatoes and steamed broccoli florets and spoon over the shrimp cream.

Turbot with peas, lettuce and bacon

I'm particularly fond of this combination of salty bacon, sweet peas and lettuce and fried fish. You can use cos or romaine lettuce instead of little gem, or even iceberg at a push. If fresh peas aren't available, then frozen petit pois make a good substitute. The garnish should be soupy, so I like to serve this in shallow bowls. The garnish also works well with other firm-fleshed fish, such as halibut, monkfish, John Dory or brill.

1 tablespoon sunflower oil

1 tablespoon Clarified Butter (see page 186)

4 x 175g/6oz turbot fillets

freshly squeezed lemon juice, to taste

sea salt and freshly ground black pepper

For the braised peas, lettuce and bacon:

1 tablespoon extra virgin olive oil

50g/2oz rindless streaky bacon or pancetta, chopped

½ onion, peeled and very finely chopped

1 small garlic clove, peeled and crushed

350g/12oz shelled fresh peas or frozen petits pois

a pinch of caster sugar

6 tablespoons Basic Fish Stock (see page 181)

25g/1oz unsalted butter

2 Little Gem lettuce hearts, finely shredded

2 tablespoons chopped fresh chives

Serves 4 as a main course

For the braised peas, heat the olive oil in a pan, add the bacon or pancetta and fry until crisp and lightly golden. Add the onion and cook for another 2–3 minutes until the onion has softened and is very lightly browned. Add the garlic, peas, sugar, fish stock or water and some seasoning, cover and cook over a gentle heat – for 6 minutes if using fresh peas and about 3 minutes if using frozen – until the peas are tender.

Heat the sunflower oil in large frying pan. Add the clarified butter and the turbot fillets and fry over a high heat for 3–4 minutes on each side until just cooked through. Lift them out of the pan on to a plate to prevent them from cooking any further, season with salt, pepper and a little lemon juice and keep them warm.

Stir the butter, shredded lettuce and chives into the peas and cook for 1 minute. Check the peas for seasoning and then spoon the mixture into the centres of 4 warmed shallow bowls. Place a turbot fillet on top of each and serve.

John Dory en papillote with shaved fennel and tarragon butter

Finding big fat John Dory is becoming an extremely difficult and expensive business. Most fillets you can buy tend to be around 50–75g/2–3oz in weight. This recipe takes advantage of these small fillets and partners them with quick-cooking, thinly shaved fennel. The combination of fennel, tarragon and Pernod produces a heavy anise blast – just make sure your guests' hooters are nearby when these packets are opened!

2 teaspoons chopped fresh tarragon

175g/6oz unsalted butter, softened

finely grated zest and juice of 1 lemon

2 bulbs of Florence fennel

8 John Dory fillets, each weighing about 75g/3oz, skinned

4 teaspoons Pernod

olive oil

sea salt and freshly ground black pepper

Serves 4 as a main course

Preheat the oven to 190°C/375°F/gas mark 5.

Beat the tarragon into the softened butter, then add half the lemon zest and a squeeze of lemon juice. Taste and season, adding more lemon juice if needed.

Halve the fennel bulbs and remove the tough central core. Using a mandoline or a fine sharp knife, slice the fennel as thinly as you can. Season it with salt, pepper and lemon juice and a little splash of olive oil, tossing well to coat.

Cut 4 rectangles of thick kitchen foil, large enough to wrap each fish fillet generously. Brush the foil with olive oil and lay it out on a work surface. Season the fish fillets with salt and pepper.

Divide the fennel between the 4 sheets, piling it in the middle of each sheet to make a bed for the fish. Lay 2 fillets on top of each pile of fennel and dot generously with the tarragon butter. Sprinkle each with 1 teaspoon of Pernod. Loosely bring the sides of the foil up over the fish and scrunch the edges together to seal completely, making sure the foil isn't touching the fish. Place the packets on a baking tray and bake in the oven for about 10 minutes.

Serve immediately on warmed plates, opening the packages at the table. This is good with new or baked potatoes.

Halibut with Parmesan and pine nut crust and roast tomato sauce

This is a great main course dish for a dinner party. It sounds impressive, looks impressive and tastes fab, and best of all, you get all the work done in advance.

4 x 150g/5oz skinless halibut fillets
(steaks will do)

25g/1oz unsalted butter, plus a little extra to
dot on top

freshly squeezed lemon juice, to taste

2 tablespoons dry white wine

sea salt and freshly ground black pepper

wilted spinach, to serve

**For the roast tomato sauce
(makes 300ml/10fl oz):**

3 tablespoons olive oil

600g/1lb 5oz very ripe red tomatoes or
2 x 400g/14oz cans whole tomatoes

2 large garlic cloves, peeled and sliced

1–2 tablespoons balsamic vinegar

a large pinch of caster sugar

6–8 large basil leaves

3 tablespoons double cream (optional)

For the Parmesan and pine nut crust:

6–8 slices day-old bread, crusts removed

3 tablespoons pine nuts

40g/1½oz unsalted butter

2 shallots, peeled and finely chopped

4 tablespoons freshly grated Parmesan
cheese

3 tablespoons chopped fresh flat-leaf parsley

Serves 4 as a main course

Preheat the oven to 200°C/400°F/gas mark 6.

To make the sauce, pour the oil into a large roasting tin. Cut each tomato in half and arrange the halves, cut-side up, in the roasting tin, then scatter with the garlic. Sprinkle with the vinegar and season. Roast for 30 minutes, or until the edges of the tomatoes are slightly blackened and the tomatoes are looking a bit shrivelled.

Remove from the oven and scrape the whole lot into a blender or food processor and add the sugar and basil. Blitz until smooth, then, if you want a really smooth sauce, pass through a sieve. Either way, put into a clean pan to reheat. Taste and adjust the seasoning, then add the cream, if using (do not boil once the cream is added).

While the sauce is cooking, make the crust. Whiz the bread in a food processor to make breadcrumbs. Then add the pine nuts and pulse, but only for a few seconds so that the mix stays crunchy. Melt the butter in a saucepan, add the shallots and cook for 2–3 minutes until beginning to soften. Stir the Parmesan and parsley into the breadcrumbs, then mix with the shallots and butter to a light paste – don't over-mix.

Now for the halibut. Use 25g/1oz of butter to grease the base of a roasting tin. Place the fillets into the tin, season with salt, pepper and lemon juice and cover each fillet with the pine nut crust. Dot a little more butter over the fish. Pour the wine into the pan to prevent the butter from burning. Whack the roasting tin into the hot oven and set the timer for 6 minutes, then set up 4 warmed serving plates.

When the timer pings, remove the fish from the oven. It should be just cooked through and no more. If the crust looks too pale, whack it under a hot grill for a minute to crisp up and brown. Place a fillet in the centre of each plate, put a good dollop of roast tomato sauce to the side and serve with wilted spinach. The fish is also good with Creamy Lemon Potatoes (see page 81).

tip

If you love heat in your food, make a tomato and chilli sauce. Halve and deseed a small, fat fresh red chilli and fling it into the roasting tin with the tomatoes.

Roast halibut with carrot spaghetti, lime and coriander sauce

Halibut is an absolutely top fish – it has a beautiful texture and flavour, it's easy to fillet and the bones make good stock. No scales to get everywhere either. Obviously designed by experts, this fish is readily available during the summer months – but you have to be careful not to overcook it, since, due to its low fat content, it can easily become dried out.

4 good-sized carrots, peeled
25g/1oz unsalted butter
finely grated zest and juice of ½ lemon
1 tablespoon coriander seeds, crushed
sea salt and freshly ground black pepper

For the halibut:
50g/2oz unsalted butter
4 x 150g/5oz skinless halibut fillets (steaks will do)
freshly squeezed lemon juice, to taste
2 tablespoons dry white wine

For the lime and coriander sauce:
1 quantity Butter Sauce (see page 186)
1 teaspoon lime zest
2 tablespoons chopped fresh coriander
sea salt and cayenne pepper

Serves 4 as a main course

tips

You can use a mandoline or Japanese vegetable slicer to make the carrot spaghetti, or use a vegetable peeler for a cheaper solution.

To check whether these thick fillets are cooked, poke them with your finger. Compare the springiness of the edge and centre of the fillet. When they feel similar, the halibut is cooked through.

Preheat the oven to 230°C/450°F/gas mark 8 for cooking the halibut later – the oven must be nice and hot.

Make the butter sauce. Add the lime zest, coriander and a pinch each of salt and cayenne pepper and keep it warm ready for use, but do not boil. (A small warmed Thermos flask will provide the ideal storage and allow you to make the sauce well beforehand.)

Cut the carrots into long, thin slices, then stack them up and cut into long matchsticks; or using a mandoline or other kitchen tool of your choice, slice into long julienne.

Heat the butter in a wide frying or sauté pan, add the carrots and toss to coat in the butter. Add the lemon zest and juice, coriander seeds and salt and pepper to taste. Put on a lid and leave to sweat for about 8 minutes, or until the carrots are tender. Remove the lid and give the pan a good blast of heat to drive off excess moisture and glaze the carrots. Remove from the heat and keep warm.

Now for the halibut. Use 25g/1oz of the butter to grease the base of a roasting tin. Place the fillets into the tin, season with salt, pepper and lemon juice and dot the remaining butter over the fish. Pour the wine into the pan to prevent the butter from burning. Whack the roasting tin into the hot oven and set the timer for 6–8 minutes (depending on the thickness of the fish), then set up 4 warmed serving plates.

Place 4 good-sized piles of the carrot spaghetti in the centre of each plate. Spoon the sauce around each pile of carrot. When the timer pings, remove the fish from the oven. It should be just cooked through and no more. Place a fillet in the centre of each plate – you can spoon over the juices left in the roasting tin for extra flavour – and hand them out to the lucky guests. Serve with new potatoes or mash, and a green salad.

Monkfish with spring vegetable stew

I was inspired to make this dish when our garden produced its first baby spring vegetables. This recipe is proof that healthy doesn't have to be boring. Best prepared for just two people, it's cooked in minutes and looks so fresh and appetising. You can substitute any other kind of fish for the monkfish and you can vary the vegetables according to season. You may have to adjust the cooking times for denser- or lighter-fleshed fish.

300g/11oz monkfish tail, after filleting
  and skinning

150ml/5fl oz water

25g/1oz unsalted butter

2 new carrots, scraped and diced small

2 small white turnips, peeled and diced small

75g/3oz fresh shelled or frozen peas

6 ripe, whole cherry tomatoes

75g/3oz asparagus, peeled and cut into
  2.5cm/1 inch pieces

3 tablespoons chopped fresh herbs
  (combination of parsley, chives, chervil and
  basil, or whatever you prefer)

freshly squeezed lemon juice, to taste

sea salt and freshly ground black pepper

Serves 2 as a main course

Cut the monkfish into 1cm/½ inch thick slices, cover and chill.

Take a medium-sized deep frying or sauté pan and add the water and butter. Bring to the boil and, when the butter has melted and the liquid rolling, throw in the diced carrots and turnips. Simmer for 2–3 minutes, until almost tender. Add the peas, tomatoes and asparagus and cook for 1 minute.

Uncover the monkfish and lay it on top of the vegetables, then slam on the lid and simmer for 3 minutes. Lift the lid, scatter the herbs on top, cover again and simmer for a final minute.

Whip off the lid, taste the collected juices and season with a little salt, pepper and lemon juice. Don't hang around – serve this right away with loads of crusty bread. (You could add a dash of cream at the end if you must, but the flavour of all those fresh veg and the juices from the fish are delicious enough.)

tip

The secret of success is to ensure that the fish is cut into even-sized pieces so they all cook uniformly.

Monkfish with spiced lentils

Tiny Puy lentils come from a specific area in France and are a beautiful slatey greenish grey. They have a lovely earthy flavour and tend to remain whole when cooked. All lentils have an affinity with curry spices (think tarka dhal and dhansak) and these are no exception.

Get your fishmonger to cut the fillets from two large monkfish tails and trim away all the skin and membrane so you're left with perfect white fillets. The fish should be quite bright, slightly shiny and beautifully fresh. The curried lentils don't reheat too well (they absorb too much of the sauce) so prepare them just before serving.

200g/7oz Puy lentils

400g/14oz monkfish tail, after filleting and skinning

50ml/2fl oz olive oil

25g/1oz peeled carrot, very finely diced

25g/1oz celery, very finely diced

25g/1oz leek, very finely diced

1 garlic clove, peeled and finely chopped or crushed

1.5cm/¾ inch piece of fresh root ginger, chopped and juiced through a garlic crusher

2 teaspoons mild curry paste

300ml/10fl oz Basic Fish Stock (see page 181) or Marinated Vegetable Stock (see page 184)

3 ripe vine tomatoes, roughly chopped

4 tablespoons chopped fresh coriander

2 tablespoons crème fraîche

sea salt and freshly ground black pepper

Serves 4–6 as a starter, or add some new potatoes and greens and it'll do 4 as a main course

First cook the lentils in boiling water for 20–30 minutes, or until tender. Drain them in a colander and spread out on a tray to dry.

Cut the monkfish into thin slices, about 2.5–5mm/⅛–¼ inch thick, cover and chill.

Warm the olive oil in a saucepan and sweat the carrot, celery, leek and garlic until soft – about 5 minutes. Add the ginger juice, curry paste and some seasoning and cook for 2–3 minutes. Stir in the lentils, then add the stock and bring to the boil. Add the tomatoes and 3 tablespoons of the chopped coriander, check the seasoning and simmer for 2–3 minutes, or until you have a loose sauce – not too wet, not too dry. Stir the crème fraîche into the lentils, which should be looking nice and rich by now.

Uncover the monkfish, season with salt and pepper and mix into the lentils, stirring constantly until just cooked and opaque – 1–2 minutes. Taste the collected juices and season with a little salt and pepper, then remove from the heat.

Divide the lentils and monkfish between 4 warmed serving bowls and serve garnished with the rest of the chopped coriander.

tips

I use curry paste where possible as I think the flavour is better than curry powder.

Use any type of firm-fleshed fish for this dish – halibut and cod could both be a good substitute for monkfish.

Monkfish roasted with pancetta and red wine sauce

Due to its meaty texture and fine, sweet flavour, monkfish has a natural affinity to bacon. In recognition of this meaty, bacon thing, I love this served with a red wine sauce. It's also great served with floury baked potatoes and fine beans.

400g/14oz monkfish tail, after filleting
  and skinning
a couple of sprigs of fresh thyme
10–12 thin slices of smoked pancetta
25g/1oz butter
freshly squeezed lemon juice, to taste
4 tablespoons water or white wine
sea salt and freshly ground black pepper

For the red wine sauce:
150ml/5fl oz red wine (I like a light one like
  Beaujolais)
1 teaspoon black treacle or dark brown sugar
300ml/10fl oz Basic Fish Stock (see page 181)
25g/1oz cold, unsalted butter, diced

Serves 4 as a main course

tip

Pat the monkfish fillets dry before wrapping in bacon. This will allow the bacon to adhere properly to the flesh of the fish.

First prepare the monkfish. Take the 2 fillets and season with salt, pepper and lemon juice. Strip the leaves off the thyme sprigs and roll the monkfish in the leaves. Set one fillet on top of the other, tapered end on top of fatter end. Wrap the whole thing with overlapping slices of pancetta, making sure the fish is completely covered. Using fine string, tie up at 2.5cm/1 inch intervals to make a small gigot or 'joint'. Cover and refrigerate until needed, but take it out of the fridge 20 minutes before you start cooking to allow it to come to room temperature.

Now make the red wine sauce. Bring the wine to the boil in a saucepan, add the treacle or sugar and boil until it is reduced by about three-quarters to a thick and foamy syrup. Add the stock and boil until reduced to about 150ml/5fl oz. Then add the diced butter, a few pieces at a time, swirling the pan as the butter melts. The sauce needs to be dark and glossy, so don't be tempted to whisk in the butter, as this would make it too foamy. Keep swirling the pan until the butter has been incorporated, then season the sauce and keep warm. If it begins to look as if it might split, heat it up a bit and give the pan a good swirl until you have a glossy sauce again. Keep it warm.

Preheat the oven to 230°C/450°F/gas mark 8.

Heavily grease a baking dish with some of the butter and place the tied monkfish in it. Sprinkle with lemon juice, dot generously with the rest of the butter and season. Add the water or wine and bake for 10–12 minutes, or until just cooked through.

When the fish is cooked, remove from the oven and baste with its juices, then leave to rest for 4–5 minutes.

Have 4 warmed plates ready, slice the monkfish thickly, arrange on the plates and spoon over the sauce. Serve with fine beans and baked potatoes.

Monkfish saltimbocca with linguine and crispy sage

These really do jump into your mouth as the name implies. They are traditionally made with veal, but monkfish, cured ham and sage are made for each other and a real doddle to make. Don't economise on the butter – it makes the dish.

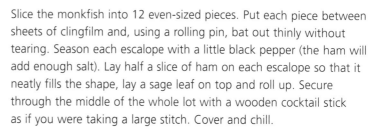

450g/1lb monkfish tail, after filleting and skinning

6 thin slices of prosciutto crudo or Parma ham, halved

24 fresh sage leaves

3 tablespoons olive oil

350g/12 oz dried linguine

seasoned flour for dusting

75g/3oz unsalted butter

3 tablespoons chopped fresh flat-leaf parsley

finely grated zest and juice of ½ lemon

sea salt and freshly ground black pepper

lemon wedges, to serve

Serves 4 as a main course

Slice the monkfish into 12 even-sized pieces. Put each piece between sheets of clingfilm and, using a rolling pin, bat out thinly without tearing. Season each escalope with a little black pepper (the ham will add enough salt). Lay half a slice of ham on each escalope so that it neatly fills the shape, lay a sage leaf on top and roll up. Secure through the middle of the whole lot with a wooden cocktail stick as if you were taking a large stitch. Cover and chill.

For the crispy sage leaves, heat 2 tablespoons of the oil in a frying pan and when almost smoking, add the remaining sage leaves. Stir around for 1 minute until they are coated with the oil and start to turn translucent and begin to crisp up but not colour. Lift out of the pan and drain on kitchen paper. Set aside, but keep the pan and its sage-flavoured oil.

Bring a large saucepan of salted water to the boil. Throw in the linguine and cook for the recommended time.

While the linguine is cooking, dust the monkfish saltimboccas with flour. Reheat the frying pan, add 25g/1oz of the butter and wait until foaming. Fry the rolls 6 at a time over a high heat for 1–2 minutes, shaking the pan so that they brown all over. Lift out of the pan with a slotted spoon to a tray and keep warm. Add another 25g/1oz of the butter to the pan and fry the remaining rolls.

Add the remaining 25g/1oz butter to the frying pan and, when foamy, add the parsley, lemon zest and juice and boil for 30 seconds.

Drain the linguine well and throw into the frying pan. Toss well to coat with the lemony, buttery pan juices. Wind the linguine around a carving fork into 4 'barrels'. Place a barrel on each of four warmed plates and set a pile of saltimboccas beside each one. Place a pile of crispy sage leaves on top and serve immediately with plenty of lemon to squeeze over. This is great with a peppery rocket salad.

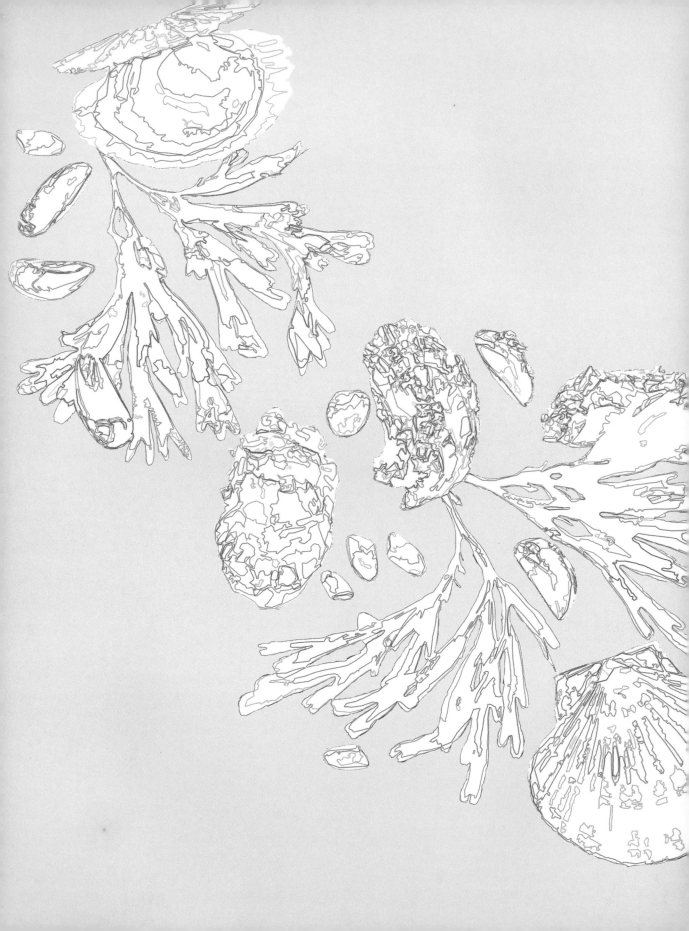

shellfish, octopus and squid

Cooking shellfish

There's a huge variety of shellfish available these days, but here we're talking about bivalves, which are filtration-feeding shellfish that live between two shells, like mussels, scallops and clams.

If you're cooking them yourself, they must be bought alive and should be as fresh as possible; if in doubt, use your nose. Really fresh shellfish should smell of the sea with a clean iodine aroma. Any whiff of fish or ammonia and they should be rejected, as they will be dead and dying and not at all good (or safe) to cook and eat. Always discard any that have broken shells; give them a good tap before cooking and throw away those that refuse to close.

You should cook shellfish as soon after purchase as possible, but all these can be stored live in a container, covered in damp newspaper or a damp dishtowel, at the bottom of the fridge, for 24 hours.

Clams

There are loads of different clams on the market, and trying to get your head round all the different names makes steam come out of your ears. To make things simple, split clams into two basic groups: small ones like vongole or littlenecks, and big ones like razor clams and quahogs. Vongole is the Italian word for any small clam like carpet-shell clams in Britain and palourdes in France.

All live clams should be soaked in cold, fresh water for 30 minutes prior to preparation, as this helps to flush out some of the sand.

Mussels

Whereas clams and cockles are still collected from the wild, mussels are mostly farmed, but it's a very natural product and they're excellent value for money.

To clean mussels, pile them into a colander, rinse well in several changes of water, then drain. Now, pull out the beards – that wee stringy bit poking out of the shell. This may seem a bit tedious and time consuming but it's definitely worth it to avoid chewing on what tastes like bits of carpet. The mussels should be firmly closed before cooking, showing that they are alive and well.

Oysters

There are two types of oysters, the most common being the Pacific. All recipes here assume that you are using Pacific, but if you're ever lucky enough to come across some of the less common Native oysters, then just prepare them in the traditional way – as for the Classic Platter of Oysters (see page 115).

Be very careful if you're planning to shuck your own oysters. I've seen some horrible self-inflicted injuries from people using everything from knives to screwdrivers. If you want to get your fishmonger to do it for you, make sure the oysters are alive and tightly closed to start with, and transport them home in a chiller bag after they've been opened. Use as soon as possible, and remember to reserve the juice. It's fantastically tasty stuff and a crime to waste it!

If you're going to have a go at shucking, start by protecting the hand you'll be holding the oyster in. Wear an oven glove, invest in an oyster-shucking glove or wrap the oyster in a thick cloth. Use a proper oyster knife, which has a guard and a rounded point, and, holding the oyster firmly, insert the knife into the hinge of the shell. Wiggle and twist the knife to prise open the shell, catching any juice in a bowl. Slide the knife underneath the flatter top shell to release the oyster. See individual recipes for more tips.

Scallops

The best scallops for all of these recipes are king scallops, which give you the biggest yield of meat, but watch out for any that have been soaked in water to plump them up. I personally don't like the roes pan-fried with the whites, but they're good for enriching sauces or for drying and grinding up to sprinkle over salads.

Cooking octopus and squid

Cephalopod is the fancy name for a class of animal that includes two very tasty specimens: octopus and squid. Don't let appearances put you off. Both provide great eating. Squid needs minimal cooking for the best texture, whereas octopus needs long, slow cooking to tenderize the flesh. Cooked to perfection, both are tender, succulent and well worth the effort. Below, I've provided some preparation instructions, but your fishmonger should be able to do all the hard work for you.

Octopus

If you're lucky enough to come across a fresh octopus in your fishmonger, snap it up immediately! To clean, turn the body inside out and pull away all the insides (you may want to wear rubber gloves for this, as you can sometimes burst the silvery ink sac) and the bendy strips that are attached to the sides to give the octopus its shape – they pull away easily. Remove the stomach sac. Rinse it all very well and turn it the right way again. Push out the beak from the centre of the tentacles, and cut away.

Squid

Rubber gloves are also a good idea when preparing squid. To prepare, rinse the squid well. Hold the body in one hand and firmly tug the tentacles with the other to pull them away from the body and remove the soft contents of the body pouch – I find it helps to squeeze the body, a bit like milking! Cut the tentacles just in front of the eyes and discard the body contents, including the weird-looking quill, which resembles a piece of plastic. Reserve the tentacles. Rinse the body pouch under cold running water. Rub off the purply membrane with your fingers and pull off the two wings.

Mussels stuffed with pesto crumbs

Stuffed mussels are a favourite of mine and there are countless variations on how to prepare them. It can be a bit time-consuming and fiddly to stuff them individually, so we avoid that here by putting them in a baking dish and scattering the crumbs over the top. You can prepare this as a simple family meal, or if you have the time you can turn it into a stylish, restaurant-quality dish for dinner parties.

150ml/5fl oz dry white wine

2 garlic cloves, peeled and lightly crushed

1.5kg/3½lb fresh, live mussels in the shell, washed and cleaned (see page 96)

1 onion, peeled and very finely chopped

2 tablespoons olive oil

150g/5oz stale, but not dried, breadcrumbs

freshly squeezed juice of 1 lemon

2 tablespoons double cream

For the pesto

(makes about 450ml/15fl oz):

3 garlic cloves, peeled and roughly chopped

200ml/7fl oz virgin olive oil, plus extra to seal

75g/3oz any combination of fresh basil, flat-leaf parsley, rocket leaves

50g/2oz pine nuts

50g/2oz Parmesan cheese, freshly grated

Serves 4–6 as a starter,

or 2 as a main course

tip

Did you know that the bright orange-fleshed mussels are female and the whitish ones are male? Both are good, but the intense colour of the former, which is also affected by diet, is an indication of superior flavour. Yes, the ladies taste best!

First make the pesto: put the garlic and oil in the food processor and whiz until milky and emulsified. Scrape down the sides with a spatula, then add the herbs and whiz until smooth. Add the pine nuts and whiz for a few seconds until they start breaking down, but are still crunchy, not smooth. Lastly, add the Parmesan, season with salt and pepper and process for a couple of seconds until mixed in. Don't over work, the pesto should have a crunchy, not smooth texture. Scrape out into a clean jam jar, cover with a film of olive oil and keep in the fridge for up to 2 weeks or freeze. (NB. Each time you use some of the pesto, flatten down the surface with a spoon and splash in some more oil before returning it to the fridge. This keeps the pesto sealed and stops it darkening and losing its freshness.)

Preheat the oven to 220°C/425°F/gas mark 7.

Put the wine and garlic into a large pan that has a lid. Put the lid to one side. Bring to a rolling boil, then chuck in the squeaky-clean mussels, slam on the lid and cook over a fierce heat until the lid starts jumping. Give it a couple of good shakes every now and then to make sure the mussels are cooking evenly. Take off the heat and check if the mussels have all opened – if not, cook for a few seconds longer. The whole process shouldn't take more than 4–5 minutes, or you'll end up with overcooked, shrivelled mussels.

Set a colander over a bowl and pour in the whole lot. Discard any mussels that haven't opened. To remove any grit, strain the reserved liquid through a fine sieve lined with muslin into the rinsed-out pan.

If you're preparing the simple version of this dish, wait until the mussels have cooled a bit, then twist off and discard all the empty shell halves. Arrange the mussels in their half shells in a single layer in a large baking dish or individual baking dishes set on a baking tray.

Fry the onion in the oil for about 5 minutes until soft. Reduce the heat, add the breadcrumbs and 4 tablespoons of the pesto and stir so that all the breadcrumbs absorb the pesto and oil, then cook for a further 5 minutes to brown the breadcrumbs a bit. Scatter this mix over the mussels, making sure they're all well covered, drizzle with lemon juice and bake in the oven for 5 minutes.

Reduce the reserved, strained mussel liquid until it starts to thicken, then stir in the cream to thicken the sauce and serve on the side in a jug.

To prepare a more stylish dish, leave the mussels in half shells and pile a little of the pesto mix on top of each. Place on a baking tray and bake in the oven for 5 minutes, then arrange artistically on warmed plates and serve with the sauce.

Mussels steamed in foil
with Café de Paris butter

A kind of moules marinières, this dish is perfect for a casual dinner party since the parcels of mussels can be prepared ahead, ready to wham into the oven at the last moment. Café de Paris butter was originally served on top of grilled steaks, but I think it works a treat with the mussels.

1.5kg/3½lb fresh, live mussels in the shell, washed and cleaned (see page 96)

4 tablespoons dry white wine

For the Café de Paris butter:
250g/9oz unsalted butter, softened

2 shallots, peeled

1 garlic clove, peeled

2 anchovy fillets, rinsed

2 teaspoons Dijon mustard

finely grated zest and juice of 1 lemon

a few drops of Worcestershire sauce

4 tablespoons chopped fresh flat-leaf parsley

sea salt and freshly ground black pepper

Serves 4 as a main course

First make the butter. Remove the butter from the refrigerator at least 30 minutes before using. Beat until very soft, pale and creamy.

Put the shallots, garlic, anchovy fillets, mustard, lemon zest and juice and Worcestershire sauce into a food processor and blitz, scraping down the sides occasionally, until well chopped. Scrape out of the bowl with a spatula and add to the butter with the parsley. Beat well to mix, then taste and season with salt and pepper and more Worcestershire sauce if you like.

Set aside half the butter for this recipe. Roll the remaining butter into a log between sheets of wet greaseproof paper, then wrap in clingfilm and place in the freezer. (This can be frozen for up to 3 months.)

Preheat the oven to 230°C/450°F/gas mark 8. Cut eight 40 x 40cm (16 x 16 inch) squares of thick kitchen foil. Double up the squares, divide the cleaned mussels into 4 portions and pile each portion in the centre of each double thickness foil square. Leave enough room for the mussels to open.

Divide the reserved butter between the mussels and pour 1 tablespoon of wine over each one. Bring the sides of the foil up and around the mussels to enclose them like a bag and scrunch the top to close – or tie with a little string. Arrange 4 shallow ovenproof bowls on a baking tray and sit a foil bag in each bowl.

Steam in the oven for about 10 minutes, or until the mussels open (squeeze the bags to find out). Serve immediately – let each person open their bag – with loads of crusty bread to mop up the juices.

tips

Use clear roasting bags instead of foil.

These foil packages are great for cooking in a kettle barbecue.

Mussel, bacon and Brie tart

Mussels used to have a bad reputation for giving you the old funny tummy. But that was back in the days when they were collected in estuaries and found growing around sewage pipes. That's enough to put anyone off shellfish. Today, they're farmed in clean sea lochs with no pollutants; they grow naturally on ropes and feed on natural planktons. You are assured a high-quality product, and no bad tums.

For the Parmesan pastry:

125g/4oz unsalted butter, diced

225g/8oz plain flour

50g/2oz Parmesan cheese, freshly grated

¼ teaspoon fine sea salt

1 egg, beaten

For the mussel filling:

1.5kg/3½lb fresh, live mussels in the shell, washed and cleaned (see page 96)

4 tablespoons dry white wine

2 tablespoons olive oil

125g/4oz dry-cure streaky bacon or pancetta, cubed

1 red onion, peeled and finely chopped

2 garlic cloves, peeled and finely chopped

4 eggs

300ml/10fl oz double cream

3 tablespoons chopped fresh chives

225g/8oz ripe Brie, rind removed, cubed

freshly ground black pepper

225g/8oz salad leaves, to serve

olive oil and lemon juice, to dress the leaves

Serves 6 as a starter

tips

Use old pulses, such as broad beans or dried peas, to blind-bake the pastry.

If short of time, you can use ready-rolled, shortcrust pastry.

First get the pastry made and chilled. Rub the butter, flour, Parmesan and salt together in a mixing bowl until the mixture has the consistency of fine breadcrumbs. Add the egg and quickly bring it all together into a dough. Flour your hands and knead this lightly 3 or 4 times until smooth. Shape into a flat ball, cover with clingfilm and refrigerate for at least 1 hour before use.

To cook the mussels, heat up a large pan that has a lid. Keep the lid to one side. Toss in the mussels with the wine. Cover and cook over a fierce heat for about 5 minutes, shaking the pan once or twice, until it is boiling well with the lid lifting and the mussels have all opened. Tip out into a colander placed over a bowl and discard any mussels that have not opened. Remove the mussel meat from the shells and set aside to cool. To remove any grit, strain the reserved liquid through a fine sieve lined with a piece of muslin.

Preheat the oven to 200°C/400°F/gas mark 6. Roll the pastry out to 3mm/⅛ inch thick and use to line a 25cm/10 inch metal flan tin, 3cm/1¼ inch deep (or 6 individual tartlet tins). Fill with greaseproof paper and baking beans and bake blind for 11 minutes. Remove the beans and paper and bake for another 8–9 minutes until lightly golden. Leave to cool.

Reduce the oven temperature to 180°C/350°F/gas mark 4. Heat the oil in a frying pan and fry the bacon or pancetta until crisp and full of flavour. Add the onion and garlic and sauté for 5 minutes until softened, but not coloured. Add the strained mussel liquor and boil fast until completely evaporated. Allow to cool slightly.

Meanwhile, whisk the eggs and cream together with the chives, then fold in the onion and bacon mix, and then the mussels. Season with black pepper. Set the cooled tart on a baking sheet, spoon the filling into it and scatter the cubed Brie over the top, pushing it into the filling here and there.

Bake the tart in the oven for 45 minutes (or 20–25 minutes for the tartlets), until just firm and golden.

Meanwhile, dress the salad leaves with the oil and lemon juice and serve with the warm tart.

Steamed mussels with chilli, tomato and basil

If moules marinières were holidaying in Italy, they'd want to end up like this. The secret to any tomato sauce is the quality of the ingredients: the better the tomatoes, the better the sauce. You can use fresh when they're at their best (in summer), but in the winter you're probably better off with a can. Always buy whole tomatoes in cans – the pre-chopped ones use inferior-quality fruit – and go for the best you can find as it makes such a difference to both flavour and texture.

2 tablespoons olive oil

1 medium red onion, peeled and finely diced

2 garlic cloves, peeled and finely chopped

1 long fresh red chilli, deseeded and chopped

150ml/5fl oz dry white wine

200–300g/7–11oz fresh, ripe tomatoes, chopped or ½ x 400g/14oz can whole tomatoes, chopped

2kg/4½lb fresh, live mussels in the shell, washed and cleaned (see page 96)

4 tablespoons chopped fresh basil

sea salt and freshly ground black pepper

**Serves 6–8 as a starter,
or 4 as a main course**

Heat the oil in a very large saucepan that has a lid. Keep the lid to one side. Add the onion, garlic and chilli and cook over a moderate heat for about 5 minutes until beginning to soften. Splash in the wine and boil hard to reduce off the alcohol. Add the tomatoes, a pinch of salt and a couple of grindings of pepper and simmer over a low heat for about 20 minutes until well reduced and thick.

Now chuck in the squeaky-clean mussels, slam on the lid and cook over a fierce heat until the lid starts jumping. Give it a couple of good shakes every now and then to make sure the mussels are cooking evenly, and to mix the sauce.

Take off the heat and check if the mussels have all opened – if not cook for a few seconds longer. The whole process shouldn't take more than 4–5 minutes, or you'll end up with overcooked, shrivelled mussels. Discard any mussels that haven't opened.

Throw in half the basil and shake the pan to mix it in. Divide the mussels between 4 warm bowls and scatter with the remaining basil. Serve with piles of crusty bread and eat immediately.

tip

Thin-leaved herbs like basil should always be added at the end of cooking for maximum flavour.

Mussels with noodles, curry spices, coriander and cream sauce

I often find that fusion food involves a real confusion of flavours, but this dish really works. I use a ready-made curry paste rather than curry powder, as the rawness of the spices tends to cook out better. Curry paste usually stays fresher and has a better flavour than the powder, which can go stale. Don't add too much – it should be very much a background flavour.

1.5kg/3½lb fresh, live mussels in the shell, washed and cleaned (see page 96)

120ml/4fl oz white wine

25g/1oz unsalted butter

2 shallots, peeled and finely diced

1 garlic clove, peeled and chopped

1 teaspoon Madras curry paste

4 shiitake mushrooms, finely sliced

175ml/6fl oz double cream

freshly squeezed juice of ½ lime

225g/8oz cooked Oriental noodles (medium)

3 tablespoons chopped fresh coriander, plus extra to garnish

freshly ground black pepper

Serves 4 as a main course

Heat up a large pan that has a lid. Put the lid to one side. Toss in the mussels with the wine, cover with the lid and cook over a fierce heat for 4–5 minutes, shaking the pan once or twice until they have opened. Strain through a colander placed over a bowl and discard any mussels that have not opened.

Remove the mussel meat from the shells and set aside to cool. Strain the reserved liquid through a fine sieve lined with muslin into a measuring jug – there should be at least 175ml/6fl oz.

For the sauce, melt the butter in a saucepan. Add the shallots, garlic and curry paste and cook for 2–4 minutes over a medium heat. Add the mushrooms and cook for a further 2–4 minutes, then add the reserved mussel cooking liquid and reduce over a high heat for about 10 minutes until the liquid becomes thick and foamy.

Add the cream and bring back to the boil. Season with a touch of the lime juice and black pepper. You shouldn't need any salt, since the mussel juices are quite salty. Stir in the noodles, the reserved mussels and the coriander and heat through gently. Check your seasoning and add more lime juice if necessary. Serve immediately in warm bowls with extra chopped coriander.

tips

Always cover cooked and shucked mussels since they dry out very quickly. To store, put them in a container, pour over the strained juice and seal tightly. They should keep for up to three days in the fridge.

Dividing this dish between bowls can be a messy business, so sometimes I cook the noodles separately, drain and toss with 1 teaspoon of sesame oil. You can then divide the noodles amongst the bowls and pour the sauce over them before sprinkling with chopped coriander.

Risotto of mussels and chorizo

This risotto is a happy marriage of Italian know-how and the best of Scottish and Spanish ingredients. This is the classic method, but you can remove the mystique from making risotto by pre-cooking and then finishing it at the last moment.

2kg/4½lb fresh, live mussels in the shell, washed and cleaned (see page 96)

200ml/7fl oz light red wine like a Tempranillo

fish, chicken or vegetable Stock (see pages 181, 184), if necessary

3 tablespoons olive oil, plus extra to serve

1 onion, peeled and finely chopped

175–250g/6–9oz Spanish chorizo sausage, diced

2 red Romero peppers, halved, deseeded and diced into 3mm/⅛ inch pieces

350g/12oz Italian arborio rice (or other Italian risotto rice)

50g/2oz unsalted butter

25g/1oz Parmesan cheese, freshly grated

1 tablespoon roughly chopped fresh flat-leaf parsley and chives, plus extra to serve

1 teaspoon freshly squeezed lemon juice

sea salt and freshly ground black pepper

shavings of fresh Parmesan cheese, to serve (optional)

Serves 6–8 as a starter, or 4 as a main course

tip

You can prepare the base 24 hours in advance by par-cooking the rice, refrigerating it, and then continuing to cook it as needed with the stock.

Heat a large pan that has a lid until very hot. Keep the lid to one side. Put in the mussels and a quarter of the wine, slam on the lid and cook over a fierce heat until the lid starts jumping. Give it a couple of good shakes every now and then to make sure the mussels are cooking evenly and cook for 4–5 minutes until the mussels open. Discard any mussels that have not opened. Shell the rest, leave them to cool and then store, covered, in the fridge until ready to finish the risotto.

Strain off the mussel cooking liquid through a fine sieve lined with muslin into a measuring jug. You need 1 litre/1¾ pints, so if necessary add a little stock or water. Return the liquid to a pan and keep it at a constant, very gentle simmer while you start on the risotto – the stock must be at the same temperature as the rice. Have a ladle to hand.

Heat the olive oil in a large frying pan, add the onion, chorizo and diced peppers and sweat gently for about 8 minutes until the onion is soft and the chorizo is giving out its red oil. Add the rice and stir it around for a couple of minutes until it has become well-coated in the oil and is beginning to toast and turn chalky, but not colour.

Add the wine and boil rapidly for 1 minute, stirring, until almost evaporated. This boils off the alcohol, leaving the concentrated flavour of the wine in the rice.

Begin to add the stock, a large ladleful at a time, stirring constantly until each ladleful is absorbed into the rice. The creaminess of the risotto comes from the starch in the rice, and the more it is stirred the more starch is released. Continue until the rice is tender and creamy, but the grains still firm and on no account chalky in the centre – this should take 20–25 minutes depending on the type of rice used.

Just before the rice is cooked, stir in the Parmesan, herbs and lemon juice and remove the pan from the heat. Stir in the mussels, cover the pan with a lid and leave to stand for a minute to allow the risotto to relax. (You may have to add another ladle of stock – you're looking for a texture that is yielding but not stiff.)

Divide the risotto between warm serving bowls and sprinkle with Parmesan, olive oil and chopped herbs. It will have been worth it.

Stuffed mussels with lemon and Parmesan

There's no denying that this is a fiddly dish, but the results are sensational. It's all about texture: crisp shell, soft cheese sauce and squidgy mussels. The mussels can also be prepared a day in advance before the final breadcrumbing and frying.

125ml/4½fl oz dry white wine

1 fresh bay leaf

48 fresh, live mussels in the shell, washed and cleaned (see page 96)

1 egg, lightly beaten

about 75g/3oz natural dried breadcrumbs

vegetable oil for deep-frying

sea salt and freshly ground black pepper

For the mussel sauce:

75g/3oz unsalted butter

50g/2oz plain flour

175ml/6fl oz full cream milk

50g/2oz Parmesan cheese, freshly grated

finely grated zest and juice of ½ lemon

Serves 6 as a starter

tips

For a crunchier coating, dip the mussels once in the egg and breadcrumbs, then dip them in the egg and breadcrumbs a second time. This helps to prevent the sauce from leaking out during frying.

If you don't have any muslin to strain the mussel juices, try an unused J-cloth or coffee filter instead.

Pour the wine into a large pan that has a lid. Keep the lid to one side. Add the bay leaf and bring to a rolling boil. Now chuck in the mussels, slam on the lid and cook over a fierce heat until the lid starts jumping. Give it a couple of good shakes to make sure the mussels are cooking evenly. Take off the heat and check if the mussels have all opened – if not cook for a few seconds longer. The whole process shouldn't take more than 4–5 minutes, or you'll end up with overcooked mussels.

Set a colander over a bowl and pour in the whole lot. Discard any mussels that haven't opened and reserve the liquid. Cover the colander with a clean tea cloth to keep the mussels warm.

To remove any grit, strain the reserved liquid through a fine sieve lined with muslin into the rinsed-out pan – you will need 175ml/6fl oz.

When cool enough to handle, pull the top shell off each mussel (the empty half) and discard. Place the mussels upside down on a tray lined with a clean tea towel, cover and refrigerate.

To make the sauce, melt the butter in a saucepan. Add the flour and cook, stirring, for a minute or so until it goes a golden colour and smells biscuity. Whisk in the reserved mussel broth and the milk and cook, stirring constantly, until boiling and very thick. Remove from the heat, beat in the Parmesan, lemon zest, a squeeze of lemon juice and black pepper to taste. Cover the surface of the sauce with clingfilm to prevent a skin forming and leave to become completely cold and set.

Turn the mussels over and dry them well. Using a teaspoon, take mounded teaspoons of the sauce – which should be thick enough to mould – and cover each exposed mussel, filling the shell. Arrange back on the tray, cover and refrigerate for at least one hour, or until the sauce becomes very firm again. This may be done up to 24 hours in advance.

Whisk the egg with a little salt until it starts to become frothy. Pour the breadcrumbs onto a plate. Dip each mussel in the egg, then roll it in the breadcrumbs and arrange on a tray. Cover and chill until ready to cook. (They should keep for about 3 hours before becoming unusable.)

Heat the oil in a wok or deep-fat fryer to about 190°C/375°F. Fry the mussels in batches of 12 for about 2 minutes until golden brown and crisp. Drain well on kitchen paper and serve immediately – they will be very hot. Warn your guests that they're getting a mussel in its shell!

Cockle vinaigrette

Cockles are a common sight on beaches around Britain, but not such a common sight in our kitchens and that's a shame, because they're a lovely, firm and meaty shellfish with bags of flavour. They live in open, sandy areas and don't burrow to a great depth when the tide goes out, one of the reasons why cockles are still frequently collected by hand. You should be able to find Cabernet Sauvignon vinegar in any large supermarket and, as with a good bottle of wine, it pays to spend a little extra for vinegar that's been aged properly in oak barrels. This dish is delicious eaten with oatcakes or soda bread and a big pile of fresh salad leaves to mop up the juices.

1.8kg/4lb cockles in their shells, scrubbed clean

4 tablespoons red wine

3 shallots, peeled and finely chopped

1 garlic clove, peeled and finely chopped

6 tablespoons olive oil

3 tablespoons chopped mixed fresh basil, coriander and chives

2 medium ripe tomatoes, deseeded and diced

6 little Peppadew peppers, drained and diced

1½ tablespoons Cabernet Sauvignon vinegar

sea salt and freshly ground black pepper

Serves 4 as a starter

Soak the cockles overnight in cold, lightly salted water.

Next day, rinse the cockles in several changes of cold water to ensure that all the sand has been purged or flushed out. Drain and discard any cockles that won't close when given a sharp tap.

Place the cockles in a large pan with the wine, cover and cook over a high heat, giving the pan a good shake every now and then, for 3–4 minutes, until they have opened. Tip into a colander over a bowl to collect the cooking liquor. Discard any cockles that remain closed.

To remove any remaining sand, strain the liquor through a fine sieve lined with muslin back into a clean pan and add the shallots and garlic. Leave to simmer for 10 minutes until the liquor has reduced to about 3 tablespoons and the shallots have softened. Add the oil and leave it to infuse over a low heat for 5 minutes.

Meanwhile, pick the cockles from their shells. Add them to the shallot mixture with the herbs, tomatoes, diced peppers, vinegar and some black pepper (but no salt). Leave to marinate in a cool place for at least 30 minutes before serving. Don't serve this fridge-cold – bring to room temperature.

Serve in little pots with bowls of salad and soda bread or oatcakes.

tips

To strain grit out of shellfish liquor if you don't have any muslin to hand, use a fine tea strainer, a clean J-cloth or a coffee filter.

If you can't find Cabernet Sauvignon vinegar, you can use any good-quality red wine vinegar.

Spaghetti with tomato and clam sauce

'Vongole' is the Italian word for any small clam, such as carpet-shell clams in Britain and palourdes in France. They make this a delicately succulent sauce, although cockles would make a good substitute, or even mussels. Don't be tempted to use seafood pickled in vinegar – it will be revolting.

900g/2lb small, fresh, live clams (vongole), well scrubbed, or 400g/14oz can shelled clams in their own juice, drained

4 tablespoons olive oil, plus extra for tossing spaghetti

2 garlic cloves, peeled and crushed

600g/1lb 5oz canned whole tomatoes, chopped

450g/1lb dried spaghetti

3 tablespoons chopped fresh flat-leaf parsley

sea salt and freshly ground black pepper

freshly grated Parmesan cheese, to serve (optional)

Serves 4 as a main course

Soak the clams for a couple of hours in cold, salted water. Then rinse the clams in several changes of cold water to remove any grit or sand. Discard any that won't close when given a sharp tap. Drain.

Heat the oil in a large pan that has a lid and add the garlic and clams. Slam on the lid and cook over a high heat, giving it a good shake every now and then, for 2–3 minutes until the clams open. Using a slotted spoon, transfer the clams to a bowl, leaving the clam juice in the pan. Discard any clams that have not opened. To remove any grit, strain the clam juice through a fine sieve lined with muslin and pour back into the rinsed-out pan.

To concentrate the flavour, boil the clam juice until reduced to almost nothing. Pour in the tomatoes and bring to the boil, then reduce the heat and simmer for 20 minutes until well reduced.

Meanwhile, cook the spaghetti until al dente as per the manufacturer's instructions, then drain and toss in olive oil.

Stir the cooked clams and half the parsley into the tomato sauce and heat through. Taste and season well.

Divide the pasta between warmed, shallow bowls and spoon the sauce over. Finish with a dusting of chopped parsley and serve. It's not traditional, but I like a sprinkling of grated Parmesan over the top.

Spaghetti with clams (spaghetti alle vongole)

This is the classic way of preparing a dish that is on every menu in coastal Italian restaurants. It's called 'vongole in bianco' in Italy because it is cooked without tomatoes. It is so simple and relies on the freshness of the clams. Shellfish like this is traditionally served with long pasta, never the short, stubby shapes. Just remember to soak the clams very well. Though you can use clams canned in their own juice, live clams are far better.

900g/2lb small, fresh, live clams (vongole), well scrubbed, or 400g/14oz can shelled clams in their own juice

450g/1lb dried spaghetti

6 tablespoons good-quality olive oil

2 small garlic cloves, peeled and finely chopped

a pinch of dried red chilli flakes (the ones with the seeds)

3 tablespoons chopped fresh flat-leaf parsley

sea salt and freshly ground black pepper

freshly grated Parmesan cheese, to serve (optional)

Serves 4 as a main course

Soak the clams for a couple of hours in cold, salted water. Rinse in several changes of cold water to remove any grit or sand. Discard any that won't close when given a sharp tap. Drain.

Meanwhile, start cooking the spaghetti according to the manufacturer's instructions.

Heat the oil in a large pan that has a lid and gently sauté the garlic and chilli. Be careful not to let them burn. Throw in the clams, slam on the lid, give the pan a shake and cook over a high heat for 4–5 minutes, shaking occasionally until the clams open. Discard any that remain closed. Add the parsley and season to taste with salt and pepper.

Drain the pasta, stir it into the sauce and serve immediately. I like a little grated Parmesan on this.

tip

Make a stronger sauce by steaming large clams open, reserving the juices and reducing to concentrate the flavour. The flesh can be chopped up and returned to the sauce.

Clams with linguine and roast garlic cream

Roasting garlic cloves in the oven gives them a fantastic nutty flavour and creamy texture, completely cooking out the harsh garlic taste. It's easier on the breath, too. I like to cook a few heads of garlic at a time to make use of the oven space. If you can get hold of dried, black squid-ink pasta, it would look and taste very glam for a special occasion instead of regular linguine.

900g/2lb small, fresh, live clams (vongole), well scrubbed, or 400g/14oz can shelled clams in their own juice, drained

one whole head of garlic (see tip)

a little olive oil

150ml/5fl oz dry white wine

450g/1lb dried linguine

200ml/7fl oz double cream

4 tablespoons chopped fresh flat-leaf parsley

freshly squeezed lemon juice, to taste

sea salt and freshly ground black pepper

Serves 4 as a main course

tip

Roast one whole head of garlic for the recipe, then put the unused cloves in a jar and cover with olive oil – they will keep in the fridge for 1–2 months. In fact, since they keep for so long it's just as easy to roast six heads at a time.

Soak the clams for a couple of hours in cold salted water.

Preheat the oven to 190°C/375°F/gas mark 5. To prepare the garlic for baking, peel away some of the papery layers of skin from each bulb. Lightly ease each bulb apart, but make sure the cloves are still attached to the base. Sit the bulbs on a double sheet of kitchen foil and bring it up to form a loose 'bag'. Pour in 3 tablespoons of water and close the bag. Seal well, place on a baking sheet and bake for 45 minutes.

Remove the garlic from the oven and open the bag, bending the foil back to reveal the garlic. Drizzle with a little olive oil, return to the oven and roast for 15–20 minutes, or until beginning to go brown. Remove from the oven and separate into cloves. The garlic will be soft. Peel the cloves or squeeze them out of the skins. Use 8 large cloves from one head for the recipe; store the others in a jar with olive oil (see Tip).

Rinse the clams in several changes of cold water to ensure that all the sand has been purged or flushed out. Discard any that won't close when given a sharp tap. Drain.

Heat a large saucepan that has a lid until very hot. Put the lid to one side. Put in the clams and the wine, slam on the lid and cook, giving it a good shake every now and then, for 2–3 minutes until the clams open. Pour the whole lot into a colander placed over a bowl. Pick out and discard any clams that have not opened. Shell the rest and leave them to cool, then store in the fridge until ready to finish the dish. Reserve the clam cooking liquid.

Meanwhile, start cooking the linguine according to the manufacturer's instructions.

To remove any grit, strain the clam juice through a fine sieve lined with muslin or a coffee filter and pour back into the rinsed-out pan. Add the cooked garlic and boil fast to reduce by half. Stir in the cream and whisk vigorously, or whiz with a stick blender, until the garlic is smooth. Bring to the boil and cook for 1–2 minutes until slightly thickened. Stir in the clams and parsley. Taste and season with salt, pepper and lemon juice to taste. Toss with the well-drained pasta and serve.

Classic platter of oysters with all the trimmings

Sadly, I've become allergic to oysters, possibly as a result of youthful over-indulgence (I don't recommend three dozen in one sitting!). So this is a treat that I've been denied, but I certainly have fond memories. A perfect oyster should have a highly visible 'frill', a good light brown or greyish colour with a white muscle, and a nice clean flavour with a firm but creamy texture. Normally oysters are only available in the colder months that have an 'r' in the name. Breeding time for oysters is in the summer when the sea begins to warm and they become milky, fat and soft. It's obvious really, but never buy open, shrivelled or black-looking oysters with suspiciously little moisture and an eggy smell – if you eat them you will never forget it.

12 fresh, live oysters in the shell, scrubbed and rinsed
4 tablespoons white wine vinegar
1 shallot, peeled and very finely chopped
cayenne pepper or Tabasco sauce

To serve
crushed ice, seaweed and lemon wedges
brown or rye bread and unsalted butter

Serves 2 as a starter

First, open/shuck the oysters (see page 96). Set the opened half-shells in a bed of crushed ice spread on a large platter and strain the collected oyster juice over them.

Mix the vinegar with the shallot. Arrange seaweed and lemon wedges around the platter and hand round the cayenne pepper or Tabasco and the shallot (mignonette) vinegar. Serve immediately with a pile of thinly sliced and buttered brown or rye bread and start slurping! Chilled white wine or champagne is a must.

tips

Oysters must always be bought live – the shells must be tightly closed, and they should be quite heavy, as they are full of liquor/juice.

Oysters can be stored for a short time in ice or under a damp cloth in a fridge drawer.

Never drink spirits before, during or after eating oysters, as this can cause a severe allergic reaction.

Oysters with sweet-and-sour cucumber and caviar

Marco Pierre White took this classy combination of oysters, caviar and cucumber to dizzy heights in his restaurant, Harvey's. However, this is my favourite way to serve oysters with cucumber – by lightly pickling the cucumber in the oyster juices and a mild sweet-and-sour vinegar; it's much easier than the maestro's version but still very good.

20 fresh, live oysters in the shell, scrubbed and rinsed

225g/8oz cucumber, peeled, halved and deseeded

½ teaspoon finely ground sea salt

2 teaspoons caster sugar

4 tablespoons rice wine vinegar or juice of ½ lemon

2 tablespoons avruga caviar (see page 44)

sea salt for setting the shells on

fresh seaweed, to garnish (optional)

Serves 4 as a starter

First, open/shuck the oysters (see page 96), reserving the juices and the rounded shell for later. Keep the oysters in a covered dish in the fridge while you prepare the cucumber. Arrange 5 of the shells in a bed of sea salt on each of 4 small plates. Garnish the salt with seaweed if you like.

Strain the collected oyster juice into a small bowl. Add the salt, sugar and rice vinegar or lemon juice and whisk well until the sugar and salt have dissolved. Using a very sharp knife, carefully cut the cucumber as finely as possible into matchstick strips about 4cm/1½ inches long. Add this to the pickling liquor, mix well to coat, cover and leave to stand for 10–15 minutes.

Pop an oyster back into each shell, then cover with a few strips of cucumber, spooning a little marinade over them. Top with a small heap of avruga and serve immediately with bread and butter.

tip

Put scrubbed and rinsed live oysters in a hot oven for 30 seconds to make them easier to open.

Deep-fried oysters in Japanese crumbs

Normally I'm not a fan of cooked oysters, but there are a few exceptions and this is one. Panko, or Japanese breadcrumbs, have a coarser texture and remain crisper for longer than ordinary breadcrumbs. Buy them from Chinese and oriental stores or online as they are very handy to have in stock. I love the contrast in textures of these juicy little numbers and I always keep the oyster juice left over from shucking to mix in with a sauce for dipping.

12 fresh, live oysters in the shell, scrubbed and rinsed

2–3 tablespoons best-quality sweet chilli sauce

1 tablespoon chopped fresh coriander

100g/3½oz plain flour

a pinch of mild chilli powder blend

2 eggs, lightly beaten

150g/5oz Panko (Japanese) breadcrumbs (see above)

vegetable oil for deep-frying

sea salt and freshly ground black pepper

Serves 4 as a starter

First, shuck/open the oysters (see page 96) and pat dry with kitchen paper. Strain the oyster juices and mix with the chilli sauce and coriander, then transfer to a serving dish and set aside.

Mix the flour with the chilli powder, salt and pepper on a large plate. Whisk the eggs in a shallow bowl with a pinch of salt until foamy. Pour the breadcrumbs onto a large plate.

Roll the oysters in the seasoned flour mixture, then dip in the egg and, finally, roll them in the breadcrumbs. The oysters can be refrigerated at this point (see Tip).

When ready to cook, heat the oil in a deep-fat fryer to 190°C/375°F. Carefully slide the oysters into the hot oil, 6 at a time, and cook until golden brown – about 2 minutes (no more). Drain on kitchen paper and serve immediately while still hot and crisp, with the oyster/chilli dipping sauce.

tip

The uncooked, breaded oysters can be covered and left in the fridge for up to 30 minutes before deep-frying.

Grilled oysters with Parmesan and Parma ham

If you're going to cook oysters at all, this is one of the best ways. The Parma ham, cream and Parmesan add a sweet and savoury richness to the creamy oysters. Get the grill red hot, as you want these to cook quickly so that the oysters are still tender and juicy while the top is golden and bubbling.

24 fresh, live oysters in the shell, scrubbed and rinsed

350ml/12fl oz double cream

50g/2oz freshly grated Parmesan cheese

4–6 thin slices of Parma ham, very finely shredded

75g/3oz melted unsalted butter

coarse sea salt and freshly ground black pepper

Serves 4 as a starter

Preheat the grill to its highest setting. Fill a large baking tray or 4 flameproof gratin dishes with a shallow layer of coarse sea salt and set aside.

Next, open/shuck the oysters (see page 96). As you open them, set the oysters in the salt – this will stop them wobbling around. Spoon 1 tablespoon of cream over each oyster, then season with black pepper. Sprinkle over the Parmesan, then the shredded Parma ham and spoon over a little melted butter.

Slam the oysters under the grill for 1–2 minutes, until the cheese is golden brown and the oysters just opaque. Serve straight away – these don't hang around.

tip

Keep the oyster juice to add to a Bloody Mary the following day.

Scallops grilled in their shell with a creamy cheese sauce and breadcrumbs (Scallops Mornay)

I'd forgotten what a truly delicious thing this is – an oldie, but a real goodie. A basic white sauce with the addition of cheese makes this a very rich dish indeed, but the mustard and lemon juice sharpen it up. Again, we don't want to overpower the scallops here. Everyone likes their sauce a different thickness, so add less milk if you like it thick. You can always loosen it with more milk if you think it's too thick.

12 hand-dived scallops on the half shell, roes and tough muscle removed

unsalted butter for greasing

freshly squeezed juice of 1 lemon

12 tablespoons natural dried breadcrumbs

6 tablespoons freshly grated Parmesan cheese

3 tablespoons chopped fresh flat-leaf parsley, to serve

sea salt and freshly ground black pepper

For the Mornay sauce:

½ teaspoon dry mustard powder or 1 teaspoon Dijon mustard

125g/4oz strong Cheddar cheese, grated

25g/1oz freshly grated Parmesan cheese

1 quantity hot Basic White Sauce (see page 188)

Serves 6 as a starter

Preheat the grill to a medium heat.

Take the scallops out of the shells and arrange the shells on a grill pan that will fit under your grill (you may have to do 2 batches, keeping the first batch warm in the oven). Lightly butter the shells. Slice each scallop into 3 around its equator and toss the whole lot in just enough lemon juice and pepper to season them lightly. Arrange 3 overlapping slices in each shell.

For the Mornay sauce, beat the mustard and cheeses into the hot white sauce, taste and season.

Mix the breadcrumbs and Parmesan together. Spoon the sauce evenly over the scallops to completely cover them, sprinkle with the breadcrumb mix and grill for 4–6 minutes until browned and bubbling and the scallops are just cooked. Cool for a minute, then add a good sprinkling of chopped parsley and serve.

tips

Always check that the tough little white muscle has been taken off the side of the scallops.

Don't boil the sauce once the cheeses have been added – it can split and go stringy.

Seared scallops with mango salsa and sweet chilli dressing

This is a lovely combination of roast sweet scallops with fragrant salsa and a chilli kick. Delicious.

12 hand-dived scallops, white meat only

freshly squeezed lemon juice, to taste

4 tablespoons roughly chopped fresh coriander

sea salt and freshly ground black pepper

For the mango salsa:

1 large, very ripe mango

16 cherry tomatoes, halved, or quartered if large

½ medium red onion, peeled and finely diced

1–2 fresh green chillies (depending how hot you like it), halved, deseeded and shredded or chopped

freshly squeezed juice of 1 lime

For the sweet chilli dressing:

2 tablespoons light sesame oil

3 tablespoons sweet chilli sauce

2 tablespoons rice wine vinegar

Serves 4 as a starter

First make the salsa. To prepare the mango place it on a chopping board and cut a thin slice off the top and bottom. This allows the mango to sit up on the board. Now, use a sharp knife to peel away the skin, or if necessary, you can use a peeler. You will now have a skinless mango. Cut down vertically on either side of the stone, which runs lengthways, and then pare away the remaining mango left clinging to the stone. Cut the flesh into 2.5cm/1 inch pieces. Add the tomatoes, onion, green chillies, a good squeeze of lime juice and salt and pepper.

To make the chilli dressing, simply whisk all the ingredients together and season with salt and pepper.

Heat a non-stick frying pan and sear the scallops over a high heat until golden brown on both ends – this should only take 2–3 minutes. Season with salt, pepper and a little lemon juice. Remove from the heat.

Place a mound of salsa in the centre of 4 warmed dinner plates and surround with the scallops. Drizzle with chilli dressing, scatter with plenty of chopped coriander and serve.

tip

Try not to move the scallops around the frying pan before you turn them – they need to sit and caramelise in their own juices.

Mousseline of scallops with avruga and chive cream

Mousselines seem to have fallen from favour, but made properly from spanking fresh ingredients, they can be delightfully flavoursome, smooth, light, delicate and melt in the mouth.

To make scallops go a bit further, I use a mixture of scallops and lemon sole, which gives the right texture and flavour. If you're feeling flush, this really is the bee's knees made entirely with scallops.

For the mousseline:

250g/9oz hand-dived scallops, white meat only (see Tips), roughly chopped and chilled

250g/9oz skinless sole fillets, roughly chopped and chilled

2 egg whites, chilled

350ml/12fl oz double cream, chilled

freshly squeezed lemon juice, to taste

melted unsalted butter for greasing

sea salt and freshly ground black pepper

For the chive cream:

1 quantity Fish Cream (see page 185)

3 tablespoons chopped fresh chives, plus extra chives, to garnish

3 tablespoons avruga caviar (see page 44)

Serves 8–10 as a starter

tips

Those who like the roes can purée them in with the fish mixture.

The secret of a good light fish mousseline is to chill, chill, chill. Chill the mixing bowl, chill the ingredients, chill the mixture. Overworking the mix can cause it to split.

Before you start, chill both the blade and the bowl of the food processor in the freezer. Set up the food processor and add the scallops and sole and blitz to a smooth purée. Add the egg whites and salt and pepper to taste and blitz again for about 1 minute until smooth, stopping at least once to scrape down the sides. (Use a rubber spatula or spoonula to scrape down and remove the mix – less waste.) Lift the processor bowl off and chill the whole thing in the fridge for 30 minutes.

Put the bowl back on the food processor and, with the machine running slowly, pour in the cream until just incorporated, smooth and thick – again, stopping to scrape down. Taste, adjust the seasoning and add the lemon juice.

Preheat the oven to 170°C/325°F/gas mark 3. Brush eight 100ml/ 3½fl oz aluminium dariole moulds or ramekins with melted butter and fill with the mousseline to within 5mm/¼ inch of the tops. Set them in a roasting tin and half-fill it with boiling water, then cover the whole lot with a sheet of buttered kitchen foil. Bake for 15 minutes until risen and springy on top. If they feel a bit soft in the centre, pop them back in the oven for a couple more minutes. Alternatively, you can steam them gently in a steamer for 10 minutes. Once cooked they will sit happily for 30 minutes out of the water, but in a warm place. When ready to serve, reheat the fish cream gently, then add the chives and avruga, but do not boil.

To serve, turn the mousselines out onto the centre of warm plates, spoon over the sauce and garnish with chives. Serve immediately.

Seared scallops, tomato and chilli jam, crème fraîche and watercress

I know that everyone and their aunt has a recipe for chilli jam – this is mine. I keep a big pot of it in the fridge to use with all sorts of things – cheese sandwiches, chicken breasts, marinades and dressings, but I like it best 'straight' with big, meaty scallops. Again, this is one of those contrasts in tastes and textures – hot scallops, cold crème fraîche, crunchy peppery watercress and spicy, sweet chilli jam.

12 hand-dived scallops, white meat only
freshly squeezed lemon juice, to taste
200g/7oz washed and picked watercress
4 large tablespoons crème fraîche, chilled
sea salt and freshly ground black pepper

For the tomato and chilli jam:

200g/7oz can whole tomatoes, chopped
100g/3½oz fresh red chillies, halved,
   deseeded and coarsely chopped
5 large garlic cloves, peeled and chopped
1 teaspoon chopped fresh root ginger
300ml/10fl oz water
250g/9oz caster sugar
a pinch of sea salt
3 tablespoons rice vinegar

Serves 4 as a starter

First make the tomato and chilli jam. Put the tomatoes, chillies, garlic and ginger into the container of an electric blender or food processor and blend to a rough purée.

Transfer to a saucepan and add the water, sugar and salt. Bring to the boil, stirring constantly until the sugar has dissolved. Boil rapidly for 10–15 minutes, stirring every now and then to prevent sticking, until reduced, thickened and jam-like. Or, if you have more time, simmer over a very low heat for about 1 hour until thick (lazy bubbles), stirring occasionally. Stir in the vinegar and simmer for 5 minutes. Cool and bottle. This will keep for 3 months in the fridge.

When almost ready to serve, heat 4 dinner plates.

Heat a non-stick frying pan and sear the scallops over a high heat until golden brown on both sides – this should only take 2–3 minutes. Season with salt, pepper and a little lemon juice and remove from the heat.

Place a handful of watercress in the middle of each plate, top with 3 scallops and spoon round some chilli jam. Finish each dish with a dollop of crème fraîche on top of the scallops and a grinding of black pepper. Serve immediately.

Scallops and black pudding with chilli and lentil dressing

This dish is a fab combination of flavours and textures – sweet, crunchy scallops, rich, soft black pudding, and earthy lentils, all underpinned with some chilli heat.

4 tablespoons dried Puy lentils

8 large, hand-dived scallops, white meat only

4 slices of good-quality black pudding, about 2.5cm/1 inch thick

freshly squeezed lemon juice, to taste

4 handfuls mixed salad leaves, dressed with 1 teaspoon lemon juice and 2 tablespoons olive oil

sea salt and freshly ground black pepper

For the chilli dressing:

1 small fresh red chilli, deseeded and finely chopped

3 tablespoons sunflower oil or peanut oil

1 tablespoon good-quality white wine vinegar or freshly squeezed lemon juice

2 tablespoons chopped fresh flat-leaf parsley

Serves 4 as a starter

Cook the lentils in boiling water for 20–30 minutes, or until tender and, if anything, slightly over cooked. Drain them in a sieve while you make the dressing.

Whisk all the ingredients for the dressing together, then stir in the warm lentils – they will absorb the flavour of the dressing. Set aside.

Cut the scallops in half through their equator to give 16 discs. Season and set aside.

Preheat the grill and grill the black pudding for a minute or two on each side. Cut each piece of pudding into quarters and keep warm. (Alternatively, you can bake them in a hot oven, 200°C/400°F/gas mark 6, for 4–5 minutes.)

Heat a non-stick frying pan and sear the scallops over a high heat, until golden brown on both sides – this should only take 45 seconds per side. (I sometimes just cook them on one side when they are as thin as this.) Try to give them a lovely golden crust. Remove from the heat and season with salt, pepper and a little lemon juice.

Take 4 warm plates and set a mound of dressed salad in the centre of each. Arrange 4 pieces of black pudding and 4 pieces of scallop around each salad. Spoon the chilli dressing around the scallops and black pudding and serve immediately.

Greek-style braised octopus in red wine with olives

When a live octopus comes out of the sea, it is brown and yellow in colour (they are experts at changing colour under water). It has to be beaten and rubbed on a rock or stone to make it tender (this breaks up the nerves in the tentacles) before it is cooked. It's not uncommon in coastal Greece, Italy and Spain to see a fisherman flinging his freshly caught octopus on the ground or at a rock face before he takes it to market. It eventually changes colour to pearly grey. I sometimes add small new potatoes to the casserole, 20 minutes from the end, to make this a one-pot meal.

1 x 900g/2lb octopus, cleaned (see page 97)

2 tablespoons good-quality olive oil

2 small onions or 4 shallots, peeled and finely chopped

2 celery sticks, finely chopped

600ml/1 pint dry red wine

400g/14oz can whole tomatoes, chopped

a pinch of sugar

1 teaspoon freeze-dried oregano

1 fresh bay leaf

75g/3oz whole black Greek-style olives

2–3 tablespoons chopped fresh flat-leaf parsley

freshly ground black pepper

Serves 4–6

Preheat the oven to 150°F/300°F/gas mark 2. Put the cleaned octopus into a heavy flameproof casserole without adding any liquid, cover and cook over a moderate heat for about 10 minutes until the skin turns reddish. Lift out of the pan (reserving any juices in a small bowl) and, when cool enough to handle, cut into manageable pieces. Some cooks peel off the skin – this is optional, some do, some don't, it's just a colour thing.

Heat the oil in the rinsed casserole and fry the onions and celery for about 5 minutes until softening. Add the octopus pieces, wine, tomatoes, sugar, oregano, bay leaf, olives and black pepper to taste. Bring to the boil, then half cover the pan and cook in the oven for 2–3 hours until tender and slightly reduced, stirring occasionally.

Serve sprinkled with plenty of chopped parsley and some of that nice Greek bread with the sesame seeds on it.

tips

An octopus sold at a fishmonger's is usually ready for cooking and may be tested for tenderness by pulling at one of the tentacles near the body – it should feel fairly elastic and not too tight.

If there are no rocks to hand, just bash the tentacles several times with a meat mallet until floppy. But the easiest way to tenderise an octopus is, however, to freeze it for a few days before using. The defrosting process breaks down the cell structure.

Squid ink risotto

This is a truly spectacular risotto, the rich, black squid ink giving it a fabulous seafood/iodine taste. Tackling a whole squid may sound a bit adventurous, but it's easier than you'd imagine and very satisfying. You also get better 'bits', like the tentacles, which you don't tend to find in pre-prepared packages.

600g/1lb 5oz cleaned squid (see page 97), plus 2 sachets squid ink

3 tablespoons extra virgin olive oil

½ onion, peeled and finely chopped

1 garlic clove, peeled and finely chopped

about 1.5 litres/2½ pints hot Basic Fish Stock (see page 181)

150ml/5fl oz dry white wine

500g/1lb 2oz Italian risotto rice (preferably Vialone Nano)

50g/2oz unsalted butter, softened

2 tablespoons grappa (optional)

2 tablespoons freshly grated Parmesan cheese, plus extra to garnish

3 tablespoons finely chopped fresh flat-leaf parsley, plus extra to garnish

sea salt and freshly ground black pepper

**Serves 6 as a starter,
or 4 as a main course**

Cut the squid body and tentacles into thin rings and small pieces. Keep some of the tentacles whole if you like.

Heat the oil in a saucepan and add the onion and garlic. Cook gently, uncovered, for 10 minutes until soft, golden and translucent, but not coloured. Add the squid, 2 ladlefuls of stock and the wine and cook gently, uncovered, for about 20 minutes, or until the squid is tender, adding a little stock to the pan if necessary during cooking.

Add the rice and stir until well coated with the squid mixture and heated through. Mix the squid ink with a little stock and stir into the risotto. Begin to add the stock a large ladleful at a time, stirring gently and constantly after each addition until the ladleful is almost absorbed into the rice before adding the next. The creaminess of the risotto comes from the starch in the rice, and the more it is stirred the more starch is released. The risotto should be kept at a bare simmer throughout cooking, so do not let the rice dry out – add more stock as necessary. Continue until the rice is tender and creamy and quite loose, but the grains still firm and on no account chalky in the centre. This should take between 20–25 minutes depending on the type of rice used – look at the manufacturer's instructions.

Taste and season with a little salt and pepper, then beat in the butter, grappa (if using), the Parmesan and chopped parsley. Cover the pan and leave to rest for a couple of minutes to allow the risotto to relax.

Serve garnished with a little more grated Parmesan and a dusting of chopped parsley.

tip

If you're short of time, cleaned squid is available from most fishmongers, which also removes the 'ugh' factor when preparing them. The all-important ink sacs are packaged into little plastic sachets, which you can find in the chilled counter at fishmongers and some delis.

Tempura squid rings and lemon mayonnaise

I love the crunch of tender squid in crisp batter, especially when it's fried properly without a hint of oiliness. Try to get small squid (sweeter) and persuade your fishmonger to clean them for you. This leaves you free to concentrate on cooking the squid, which needs to be done at the last moment.

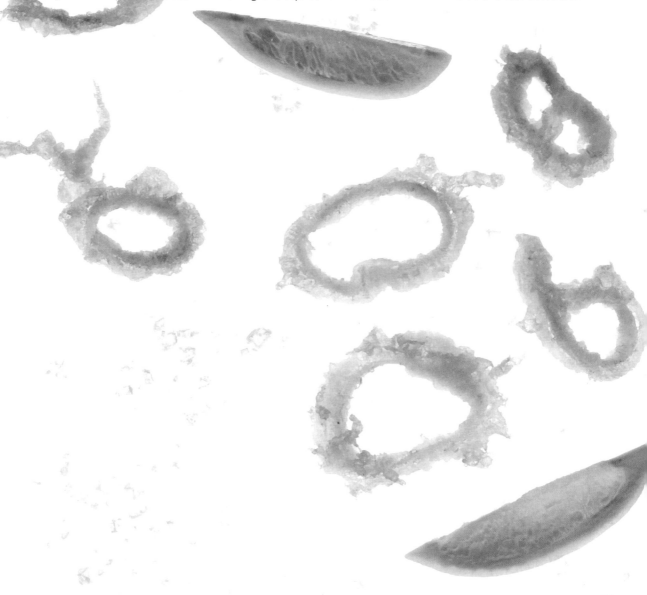

225g/8oz cleaned squid (see page 97)

freshly squeezed lemon juice, to taste

finely grated zest and juice of 1 lemon

1 quantity Basic Mayonnaise (see page 187)

plain flour for coating

vegetable oil for deep-frying

sea salt and freshly ground black pepper

sprigs of fresh coriander, to garnish (optional)

For the batter:

75g/3oz self-raising flour

75g/3oz cornflour

about 250ml/9fl oz cold sparkling water

Serves 4 as a starter

Slice the squid into thin rings and separate the tentacles if large. Season with salt, pepper and a little lemon juice and set aside.

For the batter, whisk the flour, cornflour and some seasoning together, then gradually whisk in the sparkling water until the mix is smooth and creamy and the consistency of pouring double cream (you may not need all the water). This is best used straight away, but can be kept for up to 30 minutes.

Mix the lemon zest and enough lemon juice into the mayonnaise to give a good sharp lemony flavour.

Heat the oil in a deep-fat fryer to 190°C/375°F. Season the flour with salt and pepper.

Dip the pieces of squid in the flour, then in the batter and fry a few at a time for about 2 minutes, until crisp and golden. You may need to turn the pieces halfway through cooking, so don't overcrowd the pan. Drain the squid on kitchen paper and keep warm in a low oven with the door ajar to prevent them becoming soggy, while you cook the rest.

Pile the crispy squid into shallow bowls and serve with the lemon mayonnaise for dipping. A few sprigs of coriander would work well as a garnish.

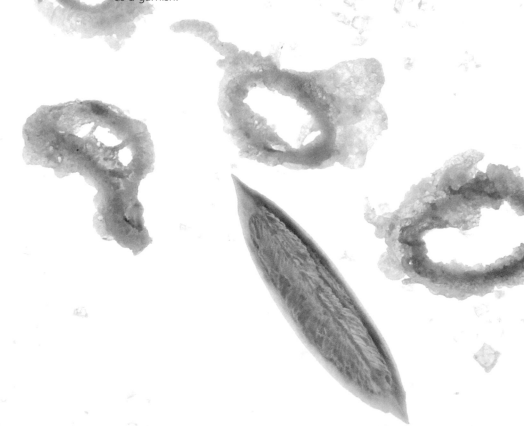

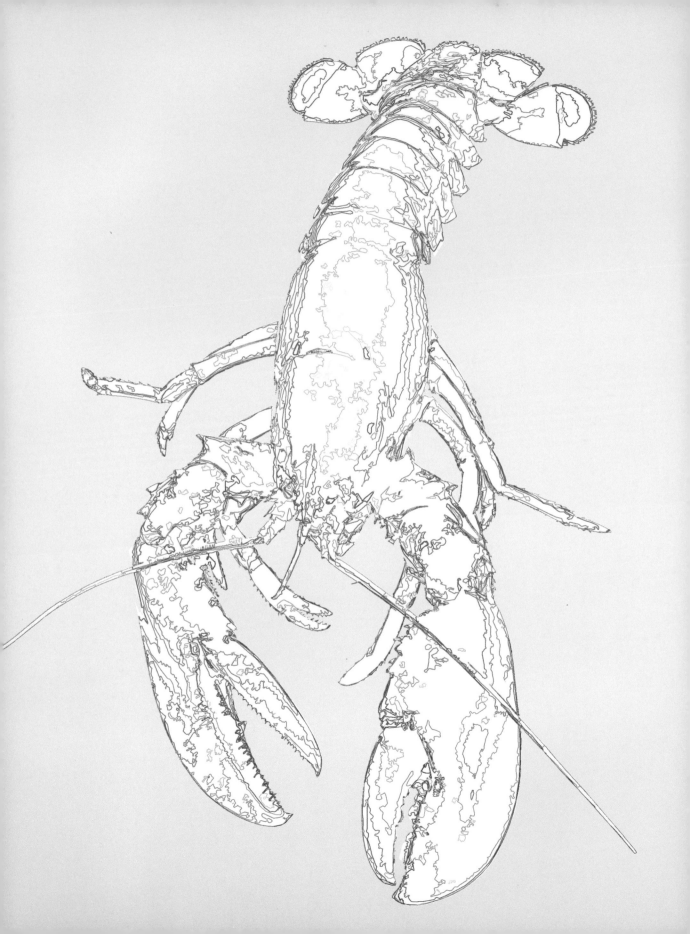

crustaceans

Cooking crustaceans

Crustaceans are basically just shellfish with legs and claws, and include the likes of lobster, langoustine and crab. All shellfish should be bought alive, and crustaceans should be dispatched just before cooking. The more squeamish among you will probably want to buy their beasts ready cooked, and all good fishmongers should be happy to oblige.

When eating cold, cooked crustaceans, such as in Salad of Lobster, Avocado and Mango Dressing (see page 172), try to avoid storing the cooked meat in the fridge since there will be significant loss of flavour. For best results, cook the lobster or other shellfish and allow to cool naturally, then serve straight away.

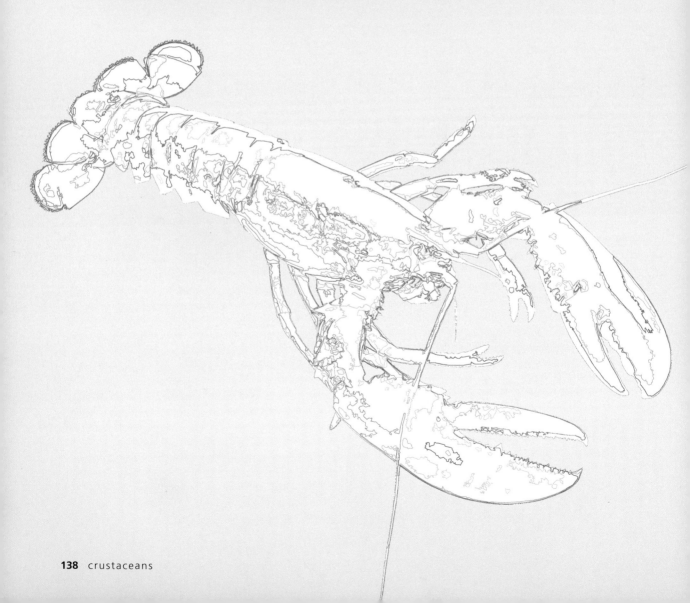

Shrimps

There's no room for argument on this one, you have to go for brown shrimps, Morecambe Bay if you can find them. They're expensive, but well worth it.

Langoustine

Most langoustines, which are also known as scampi or Dublin Bay prawns, eaten in Britain come from around the Scottish coast, and you should always try to buy creel-caught rather than dredged. I love langoustines as they have a fantastic flavour that's a world away from any other prawn.

How to shell a langoustine:

Once cooked, pull off the head. Crack the shell, or snip down each side of the underbelly with scissors, lift off the inner shell and just ease out the meat.

Tiger prawns

Cheap and widely available, tiger prawns are a reasonable substitute for most shellfish, but lack the delicacy of lobster, langoustine and crab. You can buy them cooked or raw, fresh or frozen, and they're best used in more robust dishes with strong flavours.

Frozen, peeled prawns in packets are good value. Some fishmongers buy block-frozen prawns and then turn them out for sale by weight. Such prawns risk contamination and one wonders what happens to those that are not sold at the end of the day, since frozen food, once defrosted, should be eaten rapidly and on no account re-frozen.

Tiger, Pacific or King prawns are larger than the ordinary variety and are usually sold singly in their shells.

Mediterranean prawns, which are a lovely glistening deep red when raw, are not often seen in this country. They have a delicious nutty flavour, so if you see them, buy them!

Cooking crab

A good fishmonger should be able to provide you with cooked crab, but if you're going to go to the trouble of cooking one for yourself, make sure it's as big and firm as possible. These recipes all call for brown crab and you should look for one that has big claws and feels heavy when you pick it up. If you buy a small crab you'll find it harder to ferret out all that delicious, sweet flesh.

I find that cooking crabs in a court bouillon improves the flavour, and I also cook them for a much shorter time than most people, who recommend 20–30 minutes. For some dishes you can use frozen or pasteurised crab meat instead, but fresh is always best.

To cook a crab

The amount of Court Bouillon will alter depending on the size of your crab and the size of your pan, but a 1.5kg/3½lb crab cooked in a 5 litre/9 pint pan will need 2.5–3 litres/4–5 pints of court bouillon.

1 crab, weighing about 1.5kg/3½lb
enough court bouillon (see page 182) to cover (see above)

Make sure your crab is alive when you buy it, then ask your fishmonger to kill it for you as it's quite tricky to do yourself. You don't want to cook it alive, as the legs will fall off and overcook. Place the crab in a large pan, pour in enough court bouillon to cover and bring to the boil over a high heat. Once it is boiling, reduce the heat and simmer for 12 minutes, then turn off the heat and leave the crab to cool in the court bouillon. It will be just cooked, and the meat nice and moist.

Now comes the fiddly bit. You'll need a meat hammer/mallet, old rolling pin or other small hammer, a teaspoon and, if you have one, a lobster pick (cheap to buy and very useful). Fish out the crab and discard the court bouillon. Place the crab face down on a chopping board and give its back a good bash with the heel of your hand to open it up. Pull off the claws and bash them with the meat hammer or other chosen implement. Pick out all the white meat from the claws, legs and body (the handle of a small teaspoon is useful for this, or use the posher lobster pick). This will take a bit of time, but it's fascinating to see how much you can find. Discard the feathery tough 'dead men's fingers' – really the gills – and the plastic-like stomach sac. The brown meat is found in the back shell, around the edges, so scrape it out and keep it separate. Although it looks gunky, it tastes delicious. You should get about 300g/11oz of crab meat.

Cooking lobster

There are two types of lobster: the dark blue/black European and the North American, which is greeny with a pink or orange tinge. When you cook them, both will turn that classic pink colour. I much prefer the European, but the most important thing is that the lobster should be fresh out of the sea and hasn't been hanging around in a tank. The best size is 450–900g/ 1–2lb. Anything beyond that and they start to get a bit stringy.

To kill and chop up a live lobster

Firstly, make sure that strong rubber bands are around the claws! Lay the lobster on a chopping board and steady it with one hand. Using the pointed end of a large strong knife, pierce the centre of the head where there is a cross, then press firmly all the way down to kill the lobster instantly. Split it in half along the back to the tail, cutting through both the shell and the flesh. Remove and discard the pouch of grit (stomach sac) from the head, as well as the dark intestine running along the body. Remove any coral (eggs) and the greenish creamy substance (tomalley), which can be cooked separately. Twist the joints to release the two claws from the body. Lay each half of the body flat and, using a heavy knife or kitchen cleaver, chop each into three pieces. Remove the gills from the head, close to the shell. Lay the claws on the board and, using either the broad side of the cleaver or the end of a rolling pin, bang them, one by one, until the shell is cracked at various points, so that it will not be necessary to use crackers when eating them. Cut each claw into two at the joint. And that's it!

To cook a lobster

1 lobster, weighing about 700g/1½lb
enough water to cover

Heat a big pan of water until it's boiling steadily. Kill the lobster instantly (see left), piercing through the head with a sharp knife. Remove the rubber bands from around its claws.

Put the lobster into the pan and bring back to the boil. A lobster of this size will take about 5 minutes to cook. Take it out of the pan and leave it to cool at room temperature.

To remove the meat from the cooked lobster, pull off the claws and crack with a deft blow of a blunt instrument, such as a rolling pin or a meat hammer. Extract all the meat from the claws.

To remove the tail meat, wrap the tail in a tea towel and squeeze the edges in towards the centre until you feel the shell crack. Then use the tea towel to give you purchase on the raised edges as you pull the shell apart. The shell should then split open allowing you to remove the tail meat intact.

Retain the head and shells for making Lobster/Langoustine Stock (see page 183).

Prawn paella

This is a really good dish to make for a family feast in the summer. It has some of my favourite things in it – succulent prawns, chorizo sausage and mussels. Try to use the saffron in the recipe – there really is no substitute.

In Spain, paella is cooked by the father of the family, outdoors on a wood fire in a huge double-handled paella pan. They even make big gas burners like huge picnic stoves so that you can cook it anywhere, as long as it is outside. Well, maybe our weather isn't really up to it, so give it a go inside and wash down with plenty of Rioja.

450g/1lb fresh, live mussels in the shell, washed and cleaned (see page 96)

175ml/6fl oz dry white wine

6 tablespoons good-quality olive oil

175g/6oz chorizo sausage, cut into chunks or rounds

2 garlic cloves, peeled and finely chopped

1 large Spanish onion, peeled and finely chopped

1 large red pepper, deseeded and diced

450g/1lb Spanish paella rice or Italian arborio rice

a good pinch of dried red chilli flakes

2 teaspoons sweet paprika (really fresh and not smoked)

about 1.2 litres/2 pints hot Basic Fish Stock (see page 181) or Lobster or Langoustine Stock (see page 183)

a large pinch of saffron threads soaked for 10 minutes in 3 tablespoons of hot water

12 small ripe tomatoes, halved

125g/4oz fresh or frozen peas

18 large raw tiger prawns, in their shells, heads on

4 tablespoons chopped fresh flat-leaf parsley

sea salt and freshly ground black pepper

lemon wedges, to serve

Serves 6 as a main course

Continued overleaf...

Choose a pan with a tight-fitting lid. Put the lid to one side. Heat the pan dry, then pour in the mussels, add the wine and slam on the lid. Cook over a fierce heat until the lid starts jumping. Give it a couple of good shakes every now and then to make sure the mussels are cooking evenly. Take off the heat and check if the mussels have all opened – if not cook for a few seconds longer. The whole process shouldn't take more than 4–5 minutes, or you'll end up with overcooked, shrivelled mussels. Strain in a colander set over a bowl and discard any mussels that have not opened. Cool and reserve both mussels and cooking liquid.

To remove any grit, strain the reserved liquid through a fine sieve lined with muslin or a coffee filter.

Heat the oil in a paella pan or large, deep frying pan, add the chorizo and lightly brown it all over, turning frequently. Stir in the garlic, onion and diced pepper and cook for about 5 minutes until softened. Stir in the rice until all the grains are nicely coated and glossy. Now add the chilli flakes, paprika, reserved mussel cooking liquid, the hot fish stock and soaked saffron with its water. Stir well and bring to the boil, then reduce the heat and simmer gently uncovered for 15 minutes, without stirring.

Stir in the tomatoes, peas and prawns and continue to cook gently for another 5 minutes, again without stirring.

Once almost all the liquid has been absorbed and the rice is tender, scatter the mussels on top to heat through for 2–3 minutes, then scatter over the chopped parsley. Cover and leave to stand for 2–3 minutes, then serve straight from the pan with lemon wedges to squeeze over.

Hot sweet salty sour prawn soup (tom yam)

Hot means *hot* here, so if you don't like your chillies, this may not be for you. It's not just heat you're looking for, though, but flavour, and although it should be punchy, there also has to be a balance between the chilli and the sweet-and-sour mix. The addition of coriander isn't traditional, but it adds a wonderful fragrance to the finished item.

12 raw medium tiger prawns in the shell

1 tablespoon sunflower oil

1 litre/1¾ pints boiling water

1 chicken stock cube (optional)

2 lemon grass stalks, thick white part only, finely sliced

3 bird's eye chillies, finely sliced (deseeded if you like)

3 shallots, peeled and finely sliced

150g/5oz shiitake mushrooms, finely sliced

4 kaffir lime leaves, fresh or dried

2 heaped teaspoons sugar (palm sugar, if possible)

2 tablespoons Thai fish sauce (nam pla)

4 tablespoons very roughly chopped fresh coriander

2 tablespoons freshly squeezed lime juice, or more to taste

sea salt and freshly ground black pepper

Serves 4 as a starter

Pull the heads off the prawns and peel the tails, reserving all the heads and shells. Remove the intestinal vein by cutting along the curved back of each prawn very lightly to reveal the dark vein. Flick this out with the tip of a knife.

Heat the oil in a frying pan and chuck in the prawn heads and shells. Toss them around over a high heat until they turn pink, then crush them a bit with the back of a wooden spoon to help the juices escape. Add the boiling water, crumble in the chicken stock cube (if using) and simmer for 10 minutes.

Strain the prawn stock into a saucepan, add the lemon grass, chillies, shallots, mushrooms and lime leaves and simmer for 5–8 minutes.

Finally, add the prawns, sugar and fish sauce and simmer for a couple of minutes until the prawns turn pink and curly. Remove the soup from the heat, chuck in the coriander and season with lime juice. Taste for the balance of hot and sweet and sour, adjust the seasoning and serve.

tip

A crumbled chicken stock cube added when making the prawn stock will boost the savoury flavour.

Crispy prawn wontons with oriental salad

Everyone loves these crunchy little bites – especially if they are served with this zingy salad. If you are looking for a healthier option, you can steam the wontons instead of deep-frying them. Using the wrappers is a doddle – just make sure you keep them covered when not in use so they don't dry out.

250g/9oz cooked, peeled tiger prawns

1cm/½ inch piece of fresh root ginger, peeled and finely chopped

8 canned water chestnuts, drained

a large pinch of Chinese five-spice powder

2 garlic cloves, peeled and finely chopped

20 wonton wrappers

freshly squeezed lemon juice

vegetable oil for deep-frying

sea salt

For the salad:

2 carrots, about 250g/9oz total weight, peeled and cut into matchsticks

1 cucumber, deseeded and cut into matchsticks

1 small red onion, about 50g/2oz, peeled and very thinly sliced

1 ripe mango, about 400g/14oz, peeled, stoned and sliced (see page 123)

50g/2oz raw cashew nuts, toasted and roughly chopped

1 tablespoon light sesame oil

1 tablespoon sweet chilli sauce

a good squeeze of lemon or lime juice

3 tablespoons fresh coriander leaves

Makes 20, serves 4 as a starter

Put the prawns, ginger, water chestnuts, five-spice powder and garlic in a food processor and whiz to a rough purée, then season to taste with salt and a few drops of lemon juice.

Separate out the wonton wrappers and lay them on a flat work surface on a damp tea towel. Place 1 teaspoonful of the filling in the centre of each wrapper and brush the edges with water. Pinch the sides up and around the filling to make little moneybags. Press to seal the wontons, then lay them on a clingfilm-lined tray.

To make the salad, toss all the ingredients together and arrange in a serving bowl.

Heat the oil in a deep-fat fryer or wok to 180°C/350°F. Cook the wontons in 2 batches – they will take about 60 seconds to cook. Scoop out and drain well on kitchen paper. Alternatively, arrange the wontons on an oiled plate that will fit inside your steamer basket and steam for 10–12 minutes. (You may have to do this in 2 batches if you don't have a stacking steamer.)

Place a dollop of salad onto the centre of each of 4 plates, arrange 5 wontons around the outside and serve.

tip

Wonton wrappers/skins can be found in the freezer section in Oriental supermarkets.

Classic sesame prawn toasts

Everyone loves this dish when it's cooked just right – crisp on the outside and soft in the middle. You must use raw prawns for this. Mincing the prawns with bacon or pancetta gives the paste the fat it needs to keep it moist whilst it cooks under the protective crunchy sesame crust. The water chestnuts are there for added crunch. I like to add chopped coriander to the mixture, but purists may prefer it without.

450g/1lb raw peeled prawns

50g/2oz cubed pancetta or dry-cure streaky bacon

1cm/½ inch piece of fresh root ginger, grated

1 garlic clove, peeled and crushed or grated

2 tablespoons chopped fresh coriander

1 egg white

¼ teaspoon sea salt

½ teaspoon caster sugar

1 teaspoon cornflour

2 teaspoons sesame oil

6 water chestnuts, drained and finely chopped

12 slices day-old white bread

125g/4oz sesame seeds

vegetable oil for deep-frying

light soy sauce and sweet chilli sauce for dipping

Makes about 36

Put the prawns and pancetta or bacon into a food processor with the ginger, garlic and coriander and blitz to a smooth paste.

In a small bowl, whisk the egg white with the salt, sugar, cornflour and sesame oil. Add these to the processor and blitz until you have a very smooth, slightly rubbery mixture. Transfer to a bowl and work in the water chestnuts.

Spread the mixture evenly over the sliced bread, mounding it up slightly in the centre. Cut off all the crusts. Sprinkle the sesame seeds on a small, flat tray and press each slice into the seeds to coat. Cut each slice into 4 triangles. (These can be frozen for up to one month at this stage.)

Heat the oil in a deep-fat fryer to180°C/350°F and deep-fry the toasts in batches for about 30 seconds until golden and crisp. Drain well on kitchen paper and serve immediately with the soy and chilli sauces.

tips

The prawn paste spreads best if the bread is firm and slightly stale.

I always freeze my pieces of toast and cook them from frozen – allow 1½–2 minutes, or until golden.

Coconut prawns with spicy cashew dressing and lettuce leaves

A classic combo of prawns coated in rich, fragrant coconut milk and dressed with a hot, sweet, sour, salty and crunchy zingy dressing. This all contrasts with the sweet and cool lettuce leaves for a truly mouth-watering result.

2 tablespoons sunflower oil

20 medium-sized raw tiger prawns, peeled

150ml/5fl oz coconut milk

Little Gem lettuce leaves, to serve

For the dressing:

2 tablespoons caster sugar

2 tablespoons Thai fish sauce (nam pla)

a large pinch of dried red chilli flakes

3.5cm/1½ inch piece of fresh root ginger, peeled and juiced (use a garlic press)

50g/2oz raw cashew nuts, roughly crushed

2 tablespoons chopped fresh coriander

2 tablespoons chopped fresh mint

Serves 4 as a starter, or 6 as a canapé

First, make the dressing. In a small saucepan, heat through the sugar, fish sauce, chilli and ginger juice and boil fast to reduce and thicken. Add the nuts and herbs and cook for 2 minutes, then remove from the heat.

Heat a frying pan to a medium heat, add the oil and stir-fry the prawns quickly until starting to change colour. Add the coconut milk, bring to the boil and reduce until very thick.

To serve, lay out 5 individual lettuce leaves on each of 4 serving plates. Place a sticky prawn on top of each and spoon over the dressing. Eat with your fingers, but watch out for dribbles – napkins are a must.

Vietnamese tiger prawn wraps with mint

On holiday in France I noticed that many open-air markets have stalls selling Vietnamese food to take away. One of my favourites is their rouleaux de printemps or 'spring rolls' – totally unlike Chinese deep-fried spring rolls. These are very simple, soft rice paper wraps stuffed with prawns, glass noodles and a crunchy salad of sweet-and-sour carrot and chives, mint leaves and fresh coriander. They make great picnic food, and can be made the day before and refrigerated. Get the family to help make these – it's great fun.

12 medium-sized raw tiger prawns
in the shell

75g/3oz dried rice vermicelli, soaked in warm
water for 20 minutes and drained

1 teaspoon caster sugar

1 tablespoon rice vinegar

175g/6oz carrot, peeled and finely grated

1 tablespoon chopped fresh chives

12 rice paper wrappers, about 20cm/8 inches
in diameter

125g/4oz fresh bean sprouts, blanched in
boiling water for 30 seconds and drained

25g/1oz fresh mint leaves

24 long fresh chives

25g/1oz fresh coriander leaves

sea salt

To serve:

1 small carrot, peeled and grated

1 tablespoon shredded fresh mint leaves

6 tablespoons My Basic Dipping Sauce
(see page 188)

Makes 12 small wraps

tips

Wrap the rolls tightly in clingfilm as you
make each one, to prevent the rice paper
from drying out.

For a really special treat, use langoustines
or lobster.

Bring a large pan of salted water to the boil. Drop in the prawns,
bring back to the boil and cook for 1–3 minutes until the prawns are
turning pink and just firm to the touch. Lift out with a slotted spoon
and plunge them into cold water to cool.

Bring the same water back to the boil. Drop in the soaked vermicelli
and boil for 2 minutes, or until soft. Strain through a colander, then
plunge them into cold water to stop the cooking, and drain well.

Mix the sugar with the vinegar, then stir in the carrot and chives and
set aside.

Peel the cold prawns and cut each in half lengthways along the back.
Pick out and discard the dark vein sometimes found along the back
of the prawn. Set the prawns aside.

Now you can start. Have ready a large bowl of warm water. Moisten
a tea towel or cotton cloth thoroughly with water and lay it flat in
front of you. Have everything to hand.

Using one rice paper wrapper at a time, dip it in the water to soften
– it takes less than 30 seconds. Lift it out and lay it flat on the damp
cloth. Place about 1 tablespoon of vermicelli on it, spreading them
in a line across the wrapper about one-third of the way from the
bottom edge. Lay about 1 tablespoon of bean sprouts and 1 heaped
teaspoon of carrot salad along the line of noodles and then sprinkle
several mint leaves along it. Start to roll up the filling in the wrapper
like a Swiss roll, then place 2 prawn halves along the length of the
roll. Fold over the ends to seal in the filling, then roll up another half
turn. Place 2 chives along the crease, letting one end stick out past
the end of the roll. Place several coriander leaves along the crease
and moisten the edge of the wrapper with water. Roll up completely
and place seam-side down on a tray lined with clingfilm. Cover with
clingfilm, then repeat with the remaining wraps. If not serving
immediately, wrap each one tightly in clingfilm.

For the dipping sauce, add the grated carrot and shredded mint
to the basic dipping sauce.

Serve the wraps whole or cut in half on the diagonal with some
dipping sauce.

Malaysian prawn and spinach curry

This is a well-flavoured, creamy curry, but it relies on the fragrance of a good Malay-style curry paste, which you should be able to buy in any supermarket. If you have problems, check the Web for specialist suppliers.

2 teaspoons sunflower oil

1 onion, peeled and chopped

1cm/½ inch piece of fresh root ginger, grated

1 garlic clove, peeled and crushed

1 fresh green chilli, deseeded and finely chopped

2 tablespoons mild Malaysian curry paste

1 tablespoon plain flour

4 tomatoes, chopped, or 200g/7oz canned whole tomatoes, chopped

150g/5oz plain (strained) Greek-style yogurt

100ml/3½fl oz Marinated Vegetable Stock (see page 184) or Basic Fish Stock (see page 181)

200ml/7fl oz (about ½ can) creamed coconut

finely grated zest and juice of ½ lime

1 bag of leaf spinach

350g/12oz cooked, peeled tiger prawns, defrosted if frozen

sea salt

3 tablespoons chopped fresh coriander, to garnish

basmati rice, to serve

Serves 4 as a main course

Heat the oil in a large frying pan and fry the onion, ginger, garlic and chilli until softened – about 10 minutes. Add the curry paste and cook for 3–4 minutes, then stir in the flour and tomatoes and cook for another 3–4 minutes.

Add the yogurt a little at a time, stirring well after each addition. Pour in the stock, creamed coconut, lime zest and salt to taste. Bring to the boil, stirring, then reduce the heat and simmer for 5 minutes.

Add the spinach and heat through for 3 minutes. Add the prawns and heat through for another couple of minutes, but be careful not to let the mixture boil as it will toughen the prawns.

Serve with a squeeze of lime juice, a sprinkling of fresh coriander and some basmati rice.

Potted brown shrimps

This is one of the world's best starters, but it must be served with hot, crusty toast. Too often it's all butter and no shrimps, so I press the shrimps down into the dishes a bit before covering them with the spicy butter. Avoid serving these straight from the fridge, they will be rock hard and tasteless – let them come to room temperature for 20 minutes, then they will spread onto the toast like a dream.

100g/3½oz unsalted butter

2 blades of mace or a pinch of freshly grated nutmeg

a good pinch of cayenne pepper

600ml/1 pint or 450g/1lb peeled brown shrimps

6 tablespoons Clarified Butter (see page 186)

warm brown toast, to serve

Serves 4–6, depending on portion size, as a starter

Put the unsalted butter, mace or nutmeg and the cayenne pepper into a saucepan and melt slowly over a low heat – do not allow it to boil or you will scorch the spices. Remove from the heat and leave to sit and infuse for about 15 minutes. Lift out the mace.

Add the shrimps and gently stir over the heat for a couple of minutes until they have heated through, but don't let the mixture boil or the shrimps will toughen.

Pour the shrimps and butter through a sieve placed over a bowl (reserve the warm butter). Spoon the shrimps into 4–6 small ramekins and press down gently to compact them and knock out the air. Now pour the warm butter over them, to just cover and no more. Leave them to cool completely, then chill in the fridge for about 30 minutes to set.

When they are set, melt the clarified butter and spoon over a thin layer to completely cover and protect the tops, then leave to set again.

Serve at room temperature with plenty of brown toast or crusty brown bread.

tips

You must use real brown shrimps for this recipe

You can use potted shrimps to make a great Shrimp Risotto (see page 158).

Classic brown shrimp cocktail with Marie Rose sauce

Everyone loves a good shrimp cocktail, but I have a deep loathing of the little pink slugs nestling on soggy lettuce and drowned in lurid pink sauce that many pubs and restaurants seem to serve up. For this classic dish you have to use proper brown shrimps, and Morecambe Bay ones are the best that I can think of. They're still traditionally netted – albeit using tractors rather than horses – and are still peeled by hand.

This dish has become a bit of a culinary cliché, but we all secretly love that pink mayonnaise otherwise known as Marie Rose sauce. The best pink mayo is made using the simplest ingredients, and for me that means a good-quality bought mayonnaise mixed with the best tomato ketchup. I like a dash of whisky to perk it up, and always add a drop or two of Tabasco or even sweet chilli sauce for a bit of hot spice. Serve any remaining sauce spooned over the top of each cocktail, or make extra and serve it separately for people to help themselves to more.

This is so quick and easy to make, you can assemble it at the last minute, or make it a couple of hours before, assemble it and cover with clingfilm to keep in the fridge.

350g/12oz cooked, peeled brown shrimps
2 Little Gem lettuces, finely shredded
a little sweet paprika for dusting
lemon wedges
brown bread and butter, to serve

For the Marie Rose sauce:

5 tablespoons good-quality bought
  mayonnaise

2 tablespoons good-quality tomato ketchup

1 teaspoon whisky or brandy

2 tablespoons crème fraîche

a dash or two of Tabasco or a pinch of
  cayenne pepper

a good squeeze of lemon juice

sea salt and freshly ground black pepper

Serves 4 as a starter

First make the Marie Rose sauce: mix the mayo and ketchup with the whisky or brandy and the crème fraîche, then shake in a dash or two of Tabasco or cayenne pepper, a good squeeze of lemon juice and some salt and pepper to taste. Set aside.

Mix about 5 tablespoons of the sauce into the shrimps and toss well.

Divide the shredded lettuces between 4 glass dishes. Place a pile of shrimp mix on top, spoon over any remaining sauce and dust with paprika. Garnish with a lemon wedge and serve immediately, but not too cold or you won't be able to taste it properly. Have plenty of brown bread and butter to serve with it.

tip

Brown shrimps, although delicious, are pretty expensive. To save some money, halve the amount and add in a chopped, ripe avocado and 100g/3½oz of sliced smoked salmon.

Shrimp fritters with Romesco sauce

Here at the Cook School, John Webber demonstrates these crispy, moreish Spanish snacks in his tapas class – and they have proved to be very popular, leaping straight from the pan into the mouths of students. Romesco sauce can be made well in advance and kept in a jar in the fridge. It is fantastic with all kinds of seafood. Sun-dried peppers are found in the dried vegetable section of larger supermarkets.

For the fritters:

3 tablespoons self-raising flour

½ teaspoon sweet paprika

a pinch of sea salt

2 tablespoons olive oil

125g/4oz small shrimps, potted shrimps or
    chopped prawns

1 tablespoon finely chopped shallot

1 tablespoon chopped fresh flat-leaf parsley

vegetable oil

sea salt and freshly ground black pepper

lemon wedges, to serve

For the Romesco sauce:

2 whole sun-dried peppers

1 medium red pepper

1 garlic clove, peeled and sliced

1 tablespoon chopped fresh flat-leaf parsley

½ teaspoon sweet paprika

100ml/3½fl oz red wine vinegar

75g/3oz lightly toasted almonds (of any kind)

200–250ml/7–9fl oz extra virgin olive oil

Serves 4 as a starter or canapé

First make the Romesco sauce. Soak the sun-dried peppers in hot water for 30 minutes, then drain. While they are soaking, roast the red pepper over an open gas flame or in a very hot oven and wrap in clingfilm to cool. When cold, remove the stalk and skin and deseed.

Put both types of pepper and all the other sauce ingredients except the olive oil into the food processor. Blend the contents to a thick paste, then dribble in the oil with the motor running, as if you were making mayonnaise. Add enough oil to make a thick but pourable consistency; if it's too thick add a little hot water. Set aside.

Now make the batter. Sift the flour, paprika and salt into a bowl. Make a well in the centre and pour in the oil and 6 tablespoons of cold water. Mix or whisk the flour slowly into the liquid to form a smooth batter.

Roughly chop the shrimps or prawns and stir into the batter with the shallot and parsley.

Pour about 3cm/1¼ inches of vegetable oil into a wok or deep frying pan and set the pan over a good heat. When the oil starts to haze (190°C/375°F), drop a little of the batter into the oil to test. If the oil is hot enough the batter should start to bubble and set on contact. If the oil is too cold when the batter is added, the fritters will be soft and greasy.

When the oil is hot enough, carefully drop walnut-sized blobs of batter from a spoon into it. As the fritters cook, turn them in the oil to ensure they are cooked through – about 3 minutes. When cooked, lift from the oil and drain on kitchen paper. Season with salt and serve immediately with the Romesco sauce for dipping and lemon wedges to squeeze over them – these will not wait.

tip

A wok makes a great deep-fryer for small quantities. It has a large surface area to allow the steam to release, and the sloping sides help stop the oil from boiling over.

Shrimp risotto

This is my everyday way of making a risotto for supper/tea. It may not be strictly authentic, but sometimes life is just too short for all that stirring. This more slapdash approach works very well indeed, and is a great way of making a few precious shrimps go further. It also works fantastically well with a tub of Brown Potted Shrimps (see page 153), since the butter is already infused with spices and that wonderful shrimp flavour.

75ml/3fl oz olive oil

½ medium onion, peeled and finely chopped

1 celery stick, finely chopped

1 small carrot, peeled and finely chopped

225g/8oz Italian arborio rice

200ml/7fl oz dry white wine

about 900ml/1½ pints hot Basic Fish Stock (see page 181) or Lobster or Langoustine Stock (see page 183)

250g/9oz peeled brown or pink shrimps

2 tablespoons chopped fresh chives, plus extra to serve (optional)

25g/1oz Parmesan cheese, freshly grated, plus extra to serve

50g/2oz unsalted butter

freshly squeezed lemon juice, to taste

sea salt and freshly ground black pepper

Serves 4 as a main course

Heat the oil in a large pan. Add the onion, celery and carrot and stir-fry over a medium heat until the shallot and celery have become translucent, but don't let them colour. Add the rice and stir it around for a couple of minutes until it is well coated in the oil. Add the wine and simmer for another 4–5 minutes, stirring, until almost all the liquid has been absorbed by the rice and the alcohol has boiled off.

Now lob in half the hot stock and bring up to the boil, stirring. Reduce the heat to a simmer and leave the risotto to cook until the stock has been absorbed. Add the rest of the stock and continue to cook, stirring occasionally, until the rice is tender, but with a little bite left in it, and the texture is rich and creamy. This should take 25–30 minutes in all.

Now stir the shrimps and chives into the risotto with the Parmesan and butter and beat well until nice and creamy. Season to taste with salt and pepper and maybe a squeeze of lemon, and leave to rest for 2 minutes.

Spoon into 4 warmed serving bowls and sprinkle with more chopped chives (if using) and grated Parmesan.

tip

You can use 300g/11oz potted shrimps instead of the fresh shrimps and butter in this recipe.

Shrimps with avocado and vin cotto

Vin cotto is an amazing supermarket discovery (look in the special ingredients section); it's a blend of two red wine grape juices boiled down with vinegar to a velvety sweet-sour syrup, and aged for a minimum of four years in oak barrels. It is fantastic just on its own as a dressing for avocado, but even better with sweet and salty brown shrimps, mayonnaise and avocado – long live the '70s!

2 tablespoons vin cotto

2 tablespoons mayonnaise

freshly squeezed lemon juice, to taste

250g/9oz peeled brown or pink shrimps

2 good-sized ripe avocados

sea salt and freshly ground black pepper

bread and butter, to serve

Serves 4 as a starter

Mix the vin cotto with the mayonnaise, season with salt, pepper and lemon juice to taste and stir in the shrimps.

Halve the avocados and remove the stones. Set the avocados on 4 dishes – you may have to shave a slice off the rounded bases to make them sit still. Pile in the shrimp mixture and serve immediately with brown bread and butter. It's that easy!

tip

If the avocado isn't ripe enough, put it in a paper bag in a warm dark place for a day or two.

Partan Bree (creamy crab soup)

'Partan' is the traditional Scottish name for crab and 'bree' means gravy. So this is 'crab gravy', a name that doesn't do this gorgeous soup justice. Using rice gives the soup some body and was a big thing in Victorian kitchens. It thickens everything up without using flour. When buying crabs, look for a big, heavy monster of more than 1.5kg/3½lb, which will mean less work and more meat. Failing that, you could use frozen or pasteurised crab meat, but you will lose out in flavour, both from the meat and from the crab shell, which adds its own intensity to the stock.

1.75kg/4lb cooked brown crab

600ml/1 pint vegetable, fish or chicken stock (see pages 181, 184)

50g/2oz long-grain or basmati rice

a pinch of ground mace

600ml/1 pint full cream milk

450ml/15fl oz single cream

1 teaspoon freshly squeezed lemon juice

sea salt and freshly ground black pepper

cayenne pepper and chopped fresh chives, to garnish

Serves 6 as a starter

Remove both the brown and white meat from the crab including the claw meat (see page 140) and put to one side. Put all the pieces of crab shell into a pan with the stock and bring to the boil, then reduce the heat and leave to simmer, uncovered, for 15 minutes.

Meanwhile, put the rice, mace and milk into another pan and bring to the boil, then reduce the heat and simmer, uncovered, for about 15–20 minutes until the rice is tender.

Stir all the crab meat (you should have about 450g/1lb) into the rice and milk mixture and liquidise until smooth.

Strain the crab-flavoured stock through a muslin-lined sieve into another pan. Pour the liquidised crab mixture into the stock, add the cream and lemon juice and season to taste.

Bring almost to boiling point and, if serving at once, spoon the soup into warmed bowls and garnish with a sprinkling of cayenne pepper and a few chopped chives. Alternatively, cool, cover and chill for up to 24 hours. To serve, reheat the soup, but do not boil.

Crab and sweetcorn chowder

A super supper standby using canned corn and frozen crab, this chowder can also be transformed into a fabulously decadent starter by using fresh crab and corn off the cob. Don't be tempted to use canned crab, however, as it simply doesn't have enough flavour.

50g/2oz unsalted butter

125g/4oz cubed pancetta or lardons

2 small to medium onions, peeled and finely chopped

2 garlic cloves, peeled and finely chopped

350g/12oz floury potatoes, peeled and diced

300ml/10fl oz full cream milk

750ml/1¼ pints light fish, shellfish, vegetable or chicken stock (see pages 181, 184)

2 whole corn cobs, stripped of outer green husk and silky threads, or one 400g/14oz can sweetcorn

250g/9oz freshly picked or frozen crab meat (both white and brown)

4 tablespoons double cream

a little cayenne pepper

sea salt and freshly ground black pepper

3 tablespoons chopped fresh flat-leaf parsley or chives, to garnish

Serves 6 as a starter,
or 4 as a main course

Melt the butter in a saucepan, add the pancetta or lardons and cook for about 3 minutes until just beginning to brown. Add the onions, garlic and potatoes and cook for about 5 minutes until beginning to soften. Pour in the milk and stock and bring to the boil, then reduce the heat and simmer, uncovered, for 20 minutes, or until the potato is very soft and falling apart.

Meanwhile, using a sharp knife, cut the kernels off the corn (or open the can and drain).

When the potato is cooked, liquidise the contents of the pan until smooth, then return it to the pan and whisk in the brown crab meat. Stir in the corn and bring to the boil, then reduce the heat and simmer for 6 minutes.

Finally, stir in the white crab meat and the cream, taste and season with cayenne pepper, salt and pepper, then reheat to boiling point. Serve, sprinkled with chopped parsley or chives, in warm bowls.

tip

Use both brown and white crab meat for the best flavour.

A stack of crab, avocado and tomato with tomato and orange sauce

This is a fabulous dinner party dish, full of zing, yet so simple. You can prepare it well in advance, but you must use fresh crab meat since frozen just doesn't have enough flavour to stand up to such a simple treatment. Serve at room temperature, not straight out of the fridge.

For the crab stack:

350g/12oz fresh cooked white crab meat (see page 140 for picking instructions)

125g/4oz fresh cooked brown crab meat (see page 140 for picking instructions)

about 5 tablespoons mayonnaise (good-quality shop-bought is okay for this)

2 large ripe avocados, preferably Hass

freshly squeezed lemon juice

4 ripe plum tomatoes

a dash of Tabasco (try the green Jalapeño one)

sea salt and freshly ground black pepper

4 sprigs of fresh chervil, to garnish

buttered toast, to serve

For the tomato and orange sauce:

12 ripe cherry tomatoes

6 tablespoons good-quality olive oil

2 tablespoons freshly squeezed orange juice

1 teaspoon finely grated orange zest

a pinch of sugar

Serves 4 as a starter

First make the sauce. Put the tomatoes, oil, orange juice and zest, sugar and salt and pepper to taste in a blender and whiz until smooth. Pass through a fine sieve, taste and adjust the seasoning, then set aside.

Put the white and brown crab meats in separate bowls and check over for any stray pieces of shell. Add just enough mayonnaise to each to bind together – 2–3 tablespoons to the white, about 2 scant tablespoons to the brown.

Halve the avocados and remove the stones, then peel and cut them into 5mm/¼ inch dice. Toss in a little lemon juice to prevent discoloration.

Blanch the tomatoes and peel off the skins, then halve them and squeeze out the seeds. Cut into 5mm/¼ inch dice, then mix gently with the avocado, Tabasco and salt and pepper to taste.

To finish the piles, place a straight-sided chef's ring or pastry cutter, 7cm/3 inches in diameter and 3.5cm/1½ inches deep, in the centre of each of 4 plates. Fill one-third of the ring with the avocado mix. Top this with a thick layer of brown crab mix. On top of this spoon a thick layer of white crab mix and level smooth.

To serve, surround the pile with the sauce and garnish with sprigs of chervil. Carefully remove the rings or pastry cutters and serve with buttered toast.

tips

When picking crab meat, do it over a china plate and you'll hear a 'ting' if any shell falls out with the meat.

To posh these up, top with a little avruga caviar (see page 44) or chopped tomato and a sprig of herbs.

Crab and ginger spring rolls

This recipe makes small spring rolls – ideal for 2 each as a starter, or make a whole pile and serve with drinks. They'll keep warm in the oven with the door left ajar to let out any steam, which would make them go soggy, for 15–20 minutes.

350g/12oz fresh white crab meat (see page 140 for picking instructions)

2 red Romero peppers

1 tablespoon sunflower oil

4 spring onions, trimmed and thinly sliced

50g/2oz fresh root ginger, peeled, sliced and cut into matchsticks

1–2 tablespoons Basic Mayonnaise (see page 187)

2 tablespoons finely chopped fresh coriander

1 tablespoon soy sauce

12 sheets filo pastry or spring roll wrappers

100ml/3½fl oz Clarified Butter (see page 186) or melted butter

vegetable oil for deep-frying

sea salt and freshly ground black pepper

For the dipping sauce:

2 tablespoons Thai fish sauce (nam pla)

1–2 teaspoons caster sugar

freshly squeezed juice of 1 large lime

a pinch of dried red chilli flakes

1 tablespoon chopped fresh coriander

1 tablespoon chopped fresh mint

2 tablespoons water

Makes 12, serves 6 as a starter

Put the crab meat into a bowl and check over for any stray pieces of shell (see Tip, page 162).

To roast the pepper, spear the stalk end on a fork and turn the pepper in the flame of a gas burner or blowtorch until the skin has charred and blackened; or preheat the grill to high and grill the pepper whole, turning once or twice until really blackened. Cool and then pull apart removing the stalk, seeds and skin. Dice finely and add to the crab.

Heat the sunflower oil in a small pan and cook the spring onions and ginger until soft. Drain on kitchen paper and add to the crab. Stir in the mayonnaise and coriander and mix well to bind. Season with the soy sauce and some black pepper.

Heat the oil in a deep-fat fryer to 180°C/350°F.

Brush the surface of a sheet of filo or a spring roll wrapper with a little melted butter. Keep the remaining sheets or wrappers covered with a damp cloth. Place one-twelfth of the crab mixture along the bottom edge of the wrapper, 2.5cm/1 inch from the bottom and leaving the same gap along the sides. First fold the sides in towards the crab, then the bottom edge over the crab, and roll up tightly. Repeat with the remaining wrappers and the remaining crab mix until you have made all 12.

Mix all the ingredients for the dipping sauce and pour into a small bowl.

Deep-fry the spring rolls in batches of 4–6 at a time for about 2 minutes, until golden brown and crisp. Drain well on kitchen paper and serve with the dipping sauce.

tips

Use filo pastry if you can't find spring roll wrappers. Fold the filo sheet in half to make a square before you fill.

For an authentic garnish, cut 4 spring onions into long, thin julienne strips and put in a bowl of iced water to curl up.

Crab soufflés with hollandaise

This is a savoury soufflé, straightforward to make and, as always, the secret of success lies in the preparation. To get lots of height into your soufflé, the egg whites should be at room temperature and whisked slowly, preferably by hand, to tease out the strands of albumen and prevent them snapping. Adding lemon juice helps to de-nature the albumen a little and make it more elastic and pliable, which is great for trapping lots of air and giving everything a lift.

For the soufflé:

50g/2oz unsalted butter, plus a little at room temperature to line the ramekins

25g/1oz plain flour

300ml/10fl oz full cream milk

3 egg yolks, plus 6 egg whites

50g/2oz strong Cheddar cheese, freshly grated

50g/2oz Parmesan cheese, freshly grated

25g/1oz dried breadcrumbs

a pinch of cream of tartar or a few drops of freshly squeezed lemon juice

175g/6oz fresh or frozen thawed crab meat (white and brown)

sea salt and freshly ground black pepper

For the hollandaise:

3 egg yolks

175g/6oz unsalted butter

1 tablespoon hot water

1–2 tablespoons freshly squeezed lemon juice, to taste

Serves 6 as a starter

Before starting, take six 150ml/5fl oz ramekins and put them in your fridge – this will make it easier to line them with butter. Preheat the oven to 200°C/400°F/gas mark 6.

To make the soufflé base, melt the butter in a small pan, but don't let it brown. To avoid that horrible golf ball lump, add the flour, mix well with a wooden spoon and cook for 2 minutes until it's golden brown and smells biscuity. Grab a whisk and add the milk in 3 lots, whisking well after each addition until the sauce thickens before adding the next lot. Bring it to a simmer, whisking all the time, and cook for a further 10 minutes, then remove from the heat and allow to cool slightly. Beat in the egg yolks, Cheddar, Parmesan and the seasoning and leave to one side.

Now for the hollandaise. Place the egg yolks in a metal bowl small enough to fit over, not into, a pan of simmering water. Melt the butter in another pan and pour it into a jug. Put the egg bowl over the simmering water and add the hot water to the yolks. Start whisking until the yolks thicken enough to leave a visible trace on the surface of the mix (i.e. you should see a trail of egg yolk if you lift the whisk out of the bowl). This will take 5–7 minutes.

Continue to whisk as you pour in the melted butter in a slow, steady stream. The yolks should absorb all the butter and have a beautiful, velvety texture. Now add the lemon juice, some salt and a little pepper, tasting and adjusting if necessary. Cover the hollandaise with clingfilm to prevent a skin from forming, and keep it warm until you are ready to serve.

Remove the ramekins from the fridge and grease the insides with butter, then coat them with the breadcrumbs. Place the ramekins on a baking sheet and put them back into the fridge until you need them.

To finish the soufflé, pour the egg whites into a mixing bowl, add a pinch of cream of tartar or a few drops of lemon juice and whisk, slowly at first, then gradually increasing the speed and continue whisking until the whites are nice and light, i.e. when they will stand in soft peaks. (A soft peak bends gently. If it stands straight and stiff, it's a 'stiff' peak.) It's important to not over-whisk here – if in doubt, stop.

Pour the soufflé base mix into another mixing bowl and, using a rubber spatula, stir in the crab meat. Working quickly, fold one-quarter of the whisked whites into the soufflé base and work well with your spatula to loosen up the mix. Using the spatula or a large metal spoon, fold the remaining whites in gently, so as not to knock too much air out of it – it's the trapped air that makes the soufflé rise.

Spoon the mix into the ramekins, bringing it level with the top, but take care not to get any on the rims. Give each ramekin a tap on the bottom – there's no need to smooth the tops. Place in the oven and set the timer for 9 minutes. Once cooked, the soufflés should be well risen and golden on top. They'll be a bit cracked, and some of the filling may flow out, but this is okay.

Place each ramekin in the centre of a serving plate and serve the hollandaise in a separate jug – let your guests make a hole in the centre of their soufflé and pour in as much sauce as they like. Cue applause.

tips

Soufflés a bit flat? Then twice bake them. Turn them out upside down onto buttered dishes and spoon over a couple of tablespoons of double cream. Sprinkle on some Parmesan, add a knob of butter and pop back in the oven for 5–8 minutes until browned and bubbling.

For a quicker, but thinner hollandaise, you can put the egg yolks in a blender with 1 tablespoon of hot water, and pour in the melted butter in a steady stream.

Crab cakes with garlic and chive mayonnaise

I quite often use just white crab meat in this dish, but for a real hit of crab flavour, use a mixture of both the white and brown. You must use fresh, cooked crab here, but if you're pressed for time, instead of making your own, you can use 8 tablespoons good-quality bought mayonnaise and mix this in with the garlic and chives.

For the garlic and chive mayonnaise:

1 egg yolk

1 tablespoon Dijon mustard

2 large garlic cloves, peeled and crushed to a paste with a little salt

300ml/10fl oz groundnut oil

2 tablespoons warm water

2 tablespoons chopped fresh chives

1½ tablespoons freshly squeezed lemon juice

For the crab cakes:

450g/1lb fresh white crab meat (see page 140 for picking instructions)

1 long, thin fresh red chilli, finely chopped (seeds and all)

225g/8oz fresh white breadcrumbs made from stale bread

sunflower oil for shallow-frying

100g/3½oz mixed salad leaves

a little olive oil

sea salt and freshly ground white pepper

**Serves 4 as a starter,
or 2 as a main course**

First, make the garlic and chive mayonnaise. Mix the egg yolk with the mustard and garlic in a small bowl. Using an electric whisk, very gradually whisk in the oil so that the mixture becomes thick and glossy. Spoon 4 tablespoons of this into another small bowl and stir in the warm water to thin it down into a sauce, then add the chives. Cover and set aside in the fridge.

Put another 4 tablespoons of the remaining mayonnaise into a bowl and whisk in the lemon juice. (The rest of the mayonnaise can be stored in the fridge for 3–4 days.)

Put the crab meat into a bowl and check over for any stray pieces of shell (see Tip, page 162). Fold the crab meat and chilli into the mayonnaise and season to taste with salt and pepper. Taste and add more lemon juice if you like. Shape the mixture into eight 5cm/2 inch flat discs and then roll them in the breadcrumbs so that they take on a thick, even coating. Place them on a plate or tray, cover and chill for 1–2 hours to allow them to set.

When you are ready to cook the crab cakes, heat about 5mm/¼ inch sunflower oil in a large, heavy-based frying pan. Add the crab cakes and fry them for 2–3 minutes on each side until golden. (Or, if you prefer, you can pop the crab cakes into a deep-fat fryer at 180°C/ 350°F for about 4 minutes until golden.)

Toss the salad leaves with a few drops of olive oil and some seasoning. Pile into the centres of 4 plates and place the crab cakes on top. Drizzle around the garlic and chive mayonnaise and serve.

tip

The cheat's way to fresh crab is to buy crab claws only (without the body, which is fiddly to shell) and ask the fishmonger to crack them for you.

Stir-fried lobster with spring onion, ginger and garlic

Spiny lobster or salt water crayfish (dragon prawn in Chinese) can be substituted for lobster, but the meat is slightly coarser. Cooking methods and recipes are the same for both. Only ever buy fresh live lobsters – they can be kept alive for up to 3 days in the vegetable compartment of the refrigerator, covered with damp kitchen paper or cloth.

2 live lobsters, each about 700g/1½lb

3 tablespoons groundnut oil

50g/2oz fresh root ginger, peeled and shredded

4 garlic cloves, peeled and sliced or chopped

12 spring onions, trimmed and sliced on the diagonal, white and green parts separated, plus extra spring onions, shredded, to garnish

1½ tablespoons Shaohsing wine or dry sherry

150ml/5fl oz Basic Fish Stock (see page 181)

For the sauce:

1 tablespoon cornflour

2 tablespoons water

2 tablespoons Japanese soy sauce (Kikkoman's)

1½ tablespoons oyster sauce

Serves 6 as a starter

Kill and chop up the lobsters, lightly smashing the claws (see page 141). Put the lobster pieces into one large bowl.

To prepare the sauce, mix the cornflour with the water, soy sauce and oyster sauce and set aside.

Heat a wok over a high heat until smoke rises. Add the oil and swirl it around the sides. Chuck in the ginger and garlic, stir and let them sizzle for about 1 minute until they release their aromas (don't let them burn), then add the white parts of the spring onions and toss well.

Now throw in the lobster pieces and toss around the wok until hot. Pour in the wine or sherry around the sides of the wok, lifting and stirring the whole time, and let it evaporate.

Now, pour in the stock, cover and simmer for about 2 minutes. Uncover, give the reserved sauce a good stir and pour it over the lobster, scooping and turning all the time. Throw in the green spring onion tops, toss well and tip onto a warm serving platter. Serve immediately with plenty of napkins, picks and finger bowls. Happy slurping!

Salad of lobster, avocado and mango dressing

This has a bit of an '80s feel to it, but a recent dinner party outing chez Nairn found an enthusiastic reception, so here it is.

2 small cooked lobsters, 400–500g/14oz–1lb 2oz in weight (see page 141)

2 ripe Hass avocados

150g/5oz salad leaves

olive oil and lemon juice to dress the leaves

For the mango dressing:

1 large, very ripe mango

finely grated zest and juice of 1 lime

4 tablespoons olive oil

sea salt and freshly ground black pepper

Serves 4 as a starter

First make the mango dressing. Place the mango on a chopping board and cut a thin slice off the top and bottom. This allows the mango to sit up on the board. Now, use a sharp knife to peel away the skin, or if necessary, you can use a peeler. You will now have a skinless mango. Cut down vertically on either side of the stone, which runs lengthways, and then pare away the remaining mango left clinging to the stone. Chop roughly and put in a blender with the lime zest and juice and the oil and salt and pepper to taste. Blitz until smooth. Pour into a bowl and taste – add more lime juice or olive oil to balance the flavours. If too thick, whisk in a little water.

Remove the tail and claw meat from the lobsters (see page 141). Slice each tail into 12 medallions, giving 24 in all.

Halve, quarter and peel the avocados and slice each quarter into 3 long slices. On each of 4 large plates, arrange 6 slices of avocado around the edge of the plate in a sort of sun pattern. Place a lobster medallion in the centre of each slice where the stone was.

Dress the salad leaves with some olive oil and lemon juice to taste. Add a pile of dressed salad leaves in the centre of the avocado and lobster sun, top with a lobster claw and streak the whole plate with mango dressing. Serve immediately.

Lobster macaroni with rocket

The kind of pasta you choose here is up to you – you don't have to stick to macaroni. There are masses of new shapes out there, but I love strozzapretti, which translates rather eerily as 'priest strangler' and is shaped like a rolled-up towel. This dish relies on good lobster stock and is as far removed from school macaroni as possible (though they may look similar). I served this once to a foodie pal of mine and she assured me that it was the best thing she'd ever tasted.

1 large cooked lobster (see page 141)

For the lobster sauce:

400ml/14fl oz Lobster or Langoustine Stock (see page 183)

120ml/4fl oz double cream

200g/7oz macaroni or similar pasta shape

125g/4oz fresh rocket leaves, plus a handful to garnish

60g/2½oz Parmesan cheese, freshly grated, plus 2 tablespoons freshly grated Parmesan or Parmesan shavings, to serve

freshly squeezed lemon juice, to taste

freshly ground black pepper

Serves 4 as a starter

Pull off the claws and tail from the lobster, crack them and remove all the meat. Put all the bits of shell in a pan with the lobster stock and simmer for 10 minutes to concentrate the flavour before you make the sauce.

To make the sauce, reduce the lobster stock to about 75ml/3fl oz. Add the cream and boil for 2–3 minutes until reduced and very thick.

Meanwhile, boil the pasta in plenty of salted water for 10–15 minutes depending on the pasta type. When cooked, drain the pasta well and add to the sauce with most of the rocket and mix well. Add the Parmesan, stir in the lobster and warm through. Taste and season with black pepper and lemon juice.

To serve, spoon the lobster macaroni onto warmed soup plates, top each serving with a sprinkling of the remaining rocket leaves and scatter with Parmesan. Serve immediately.

Lobster thermidor

One of our top chefs at the Cook School, John Webber, is the master when it comes to a classic lobster thermidor. But I think it is too complicated to do at home, so here is my user-friendly version. The whole thing can be prepared in advance, then popped into a blistering hot oven just before you serve. What a treat!

1 freshly cooked lobster (see page 141)

50g/2oz unsalted butter

1 shallot, peeled and finely chopped

1 tablespoon plain flour

2 tablespoons dry white wine

100ml/3½fl oz Basic Fish Stock
  (see page 181)

3 tablespoons freshly grated Parmesan
  cheese

1 teaspoon English mustard

freshly squeezed lemon juice, to taste

75ml/3fl oz double cream

2 egg yolks

1 tablespoon chopped fresh flat-leaf parsley

sea salt and freshly ground black pepper

Serves 2 as a main course

Preheat the oven to 230°C/450°F/gas mark 8 – it must be very hot.

To halve or split the lobster, pull off the large claws and set aside. Place the lobster on a chopping board and uncurl the tail so that the lobster sits straight on the board. Take a large sharp knife and literally split the lobster in two through the head towards the tail. Open out and remove the little 'plastic' stomach sack in the head. Carefully remove the tail meat and dice into 1cm/½ inch square pieces. Place the reserved, and now empty, half shells on a baking tray and set aside.

Crack the claws, remove the meat, dice and add to the rest of the lobster meat. Set aside.

Melt the butter in a heavy-based pan over a low heat. Add the shallot and sweat in the butter until soft, but not coloured – about 6 minutes. Add the flour and cook for 2–3 minutes, but do not let it colour. Splash in the wine and whisk in the stock. Bring to the boil, then reduce the heat and simmer for 3–4 minutes until it thickens.

Remove from the heat and beat in 2 tablespoons of the Parmesan, the mustard, lemon juice to taste, the cream, egg yolks and parsley. Keep 3–4 tablespoons of sauce aside, then fold the diced lobster meat into the rest and spoon into the reserved shells. Coat with the reserved sauce and sprinkle with the remaining Parmesan.

Bake the filled shells in the hot oven for 7–8 minutes until brown. Serve at once.

tips

These may be pre-prepared up to 8 hours in advance.

Should you find any bright red lobster coral or roe in the head, beat it into the sauce for added flavour.

Roasted langoustines with three sauces

When you have great-quality ingredients, you don't need to do anything too fancy with them to make a memorable eating experience. And nowhere is this more the case than with langoustines – but absolute freshness is all-important. If you are cooking them yourself, you must buy live ones, which are a beautiful deep orange colour. Dead langoustines turn a dull yellow and release an enzyme that breaks down the flesh in the tail, turning it into cotton wool. As ever, when determining freshness, the nose never lies. If you don't want to cook them, buy them pre-cooked from a fishmonger you can trust. This is a great dish to serve as a feast with friends – there has to be loud cracking and slurping noises, or the whole idea is a failure. It's best to have some 'cracky' claws for cracking the claws, but I often use nutcrackers and toothpicks. Finger bowls and a bowl for the empty shells all help the theatre of this dish. I like to serve these with a variety of dipping sauces, but you could get away with two, or even one.

900g/2lb live langoustines or 225g/8oz
    cooked and peeled fresh tiger prawns
4 tablespoons olive oil
sea salt and freshly ground black pepper

Serves 4 as a starter

For the Vietnamese dipping sauce:

4 tablespoons rice wine vinegar

4 tablespoons Thai fish sauce (nam pla)

2 tablespoons caster sugar

1 small, fresh chilli, deseeded and chopped

2 teaspoons grated fresh root ginger or
    ginger juice (pressed through a garlic press)

2 tablespoons water

2 tablespoons mixed chopped fresh coriander
    and mint

For the Sauce Verte (makes 150ml/5fl oz):

75g/3oz mixed fresh herbs

150ml/5fl oz Basic Mayonnaise (see page 187)
    or good-quality shop-bought

For the garlic butter:

100g/3½oz unsalted butter

1 large garlic clove (or more if you like),
    peeled and well crushed

finely grated zest of ½ lemon

2 tablespoons freshly squeezed lemon juice

1 tablespoon chopped fresh flat-leaf parsley

All the sauces may be made up to 24 hours in advance. Serve the Vietnamese sauce and the mayonnaise from the fridge, but heat through the garlic butter in a pan or the microwave before serving.

Put all the ingredients for the Vietnamese sauce, except the coriander and mint, in a small pan, bring to the boil and boil for 1 minute. Cool, then stir in the coriander and mint and set aside, or chill in the fridge.

To make the Sauce Verte, pick over the herbs and strip the leaves from the stalks – you should end up with about 75g/3oz. Wash and dry them on kitchen paper. Dollop the mayonnaise into a liquidizer, add the herbs and blitz until smooth and creamy. Taste and season with salt and pepper, then put to one side, or chill in the fridge.

To make the garlic butter, gently melt the butter with the garlic and lemon zest. Cook very slowly for 3 minutes to take some of the harshness from the garlic, then add the lemon juice and a little seasoning. Set aside until ready to use. To serve, reheat the garlic butter until just boiling, add the parsley and pour into a warm bowl.

To poach the live langoustines, have a large pan of boiling water ready on a fierce heat. Drop in the langoustines, slam on a lid, bring back to the boil and cook for 2 minutes. Using a slotted spoon, transfer them straight to a big bowl. Alternatively, preheat the oven to 220°C/425°F/gas mark 7. Rub the langoustines with olive oil and place in a roasting tin in a hot oven for 7–8 minutes.

If cooking in advance, cool the langoustines in iced water, drain and, if possible, avoid refrigeration before serving. If, however, you need to do this well in advance, they will keep for up to 24 hours in the fridge. Bring back to room temperature before serving.

Serve with the 3 dipping sauces.

tip

I think the tastiest flesh is in the claws.

Roasted langoustines with avocado salsa

Roasting langoustines is by far the tastiest way of cooking them, but don't overcrowd the roasting tin. You need to allow the heat to penetrate evenly and cook the langoustines at an even rate.

12 medium-sized live langoustines

4 tablespoons olive oil

For the avocado salsa:

2 teaspoons Thai fish sauce (nam pla)

finely grated zest and juice of ½ lime

1 tablespoon sunflower oil

1 large ripe Hass avocado, peeled, stoned and chopped

1 fresh red chilli, very finely chopped

3 tablespoons chopped fresh coriander

To serve:

mixed salad leaves

sunflower oil

freshly squeezed lemon juice, to taste

Serves 4 as a starter

To make the salsa, whisk the fish sauce, lime zest and juice and sunflower oil together. Fold in the avocado, chilli and coriander, then cover and leave for 1 hour to allow the flavours to develop.

Preheat the oven to 220°C/425°F/gas mark 7.

Rub the langoustines with the olive oil, place in a roasting tin and cook in the oven for 7–8 minutes.

When cooked, allow them to cool, then carefully cut off the heads and reserve. Shell them and cut the tail meat in half lengthways.

Next, turn the heads upside down and lift off the pelvis and legs. Scoop out all the soft brown meat from the langoustine heads (this is similar to the brown meat on a lobster). You should be left with a cup full of soft brown goo, but be careful not to scrape so hard that you remove the hard stomach as well. Add this meat to the salsa and mix well.

Place a metal chef's ring in the centre of each plate. Add 2 tail halves flat-side down at the bottom of the ring, then a spoonful of salsa, another 2 tail halves, more salsa and a final pair of tail halves. Press down gently so that it all merges together and the salsa acts like cement to hold the langoustine tails together in a tower.

Dress the leaves with sunflower oil and lemon juice to taste.

Carefully remove the mousse ring and top each tower with a small ball of salad leaves. Serve immediately.

tip

If you have several rings, you can make these up to 12 hours in advance, then store on a tray in the fridge and lift off with a spatula to serve. Allow to come to room temperature before serving.

Sautéed langoustines with fennel cream

This dish involves French flavours and Asian cooking techniques, producing a kind of prawny stroganoff that is as tasty as it is easy to prepare. Keeping the shells on boosts the flavours, but remember to remove them before eating.

1kg/2¼lb live langoustines

50g/2oz unsalted butter

1 fennel bulb, halved, cored and finely shaved

2 tablespoons Pernod

300ml/10fl oz double cream

finely grated zest and juice of 1 lemon

sea salt and freshly ground black pepper

2 tablespoons chopped fresh chervil, to garnish

Serves 4 as a main course

First prepare the langoustines. Using a large sharp knife and a sure hand, stretch each langoustine out on a chopping board and split right down the middle in one clean go. Open out the langoustine and remove any sign of black intestine. Bash the claws to break them so that the juices will come out into the pan as you cook them.

Heat a wok over a medium heat and add the butter. When foaming, add the fennel and toss well to coat in the butter. Cook for a couple of minutes, then fling in the langoustines and turn up the heat. Stir-fry for 1 minute, splash in the Pernod around the sides of the wok and tip into the gas flame to set alight (or use a match). Allow the flames to die back naturally, shaking the pan a couple of times.
Pour in the cream and bring to the boil, then add the lemon zest and boil for 1 minute. Toss well, taste and season with salt, pepper and lemon juice. Scatter with the chervil and serve immediately with new potatoes or steamed basmati rice.

tips

Don't have the heat too high to begin with, as the butter can burn.

Use a mandolin to slice the fennel.

Court bouillon

This is not a stock, but a really useful cooking medium, used for poaching fish like salmon and skate, and cooking crab and lobster. After using it to cook fish, I always strain it and keep it for re-use as a stock or soup base.

1.2 litres/2 pints water

½ lemon, sliced

1 small onion, peeled and sliced (optional)

1 carrot, peeled and sliced

1 celery stick, sliced

1 fresh bay leaf

15 white peppercorns

a handful of bruised parsley stalks (you can add other herb stalks, but too much can be overpowering)

Make about 1.2 litres/2 pints

Put all the ingredients into a large saucepan and bring slowly to the boil. Turn off the heat and allow it to cool. Once cold, strain and use as needed.

It can be either used immediately, covered and chilled in the fridge for up to 3 days, or frozen for up to 3 months.

Lobster or langoustine stock

This may seem like a bit of a faff, but it's well worth the effort and absolutely essential for dishes like my Lobster Macaroni with Rocket (see page 174).

3 tablespoons olive oil

1kg/2¼lb lobster or langoustine heads, preferably spanking fresh

1 onion, peeled and chopped

1 carrot, peeled and chopped

1 celery stick, chopped

2 tomatoes, chopped

1 head of garlic, sliced in half across its equator and chopped (skin and all)

1 tablespoon tomato purée

2 star anise

1 teaspoon fennel seeds

1 teaspoon coriander seeds

200ml/7fl oz dry white wine

2 litres/3½ pints Basic Fish Stock (see page 181)

Makes about 2.5 litres/4 pints

Heat a large, heavy-based pan over a high heat and add the oil. Throw in the lobster or langoustine heads and stir around the pan for 4–5 minutes until they start to caramelise and turn golden brown.

Add the chopped vegetables, garlic, tomato purée, star anise and fennel and coriander seeds, give it a good stir and sauté for 5 minutes. Pour in the wine, bring to the boil and boil for 1 minute. Pour in the stock and bring to the boil again, then reduce the heat and simmer, uncovered, for 40 minutes.

Allow to cool without straining it. Once cold, strain through a fine sieve or double muslin and discard the debris. It can be either used immediately, covered and chilled in the fridge for up to 2 days, or frozen for up to 3 months.

Marinated vegetable stock (nage)

Make big batches of this useful stock when you can. It freezes well and the ingredients are always reasonably easy to get hold of. Don't confuse this with a court bouillon – this is a proper, well-flavoured stock for making sauces and soups. Leaving the vegetables to marinate for a couple of days and then straining off the stock gives a wonderful rich, sweet flavour that I think works well with most fish dishes.

1 large onion, peeled and chopped

1 leek, chopped

2 celery sticks, chopped

1 fennel bulb, chopped (optional, but a very good addition)

4 large carrots, peeled and chopped

1 head of garlic, sliced in half across its equator

8 white peppercorns, crushed

1 teaspoon coriander seeds

1 star anise

1 fresh bay leaf

40g/1½oz mixed fresh herbs

300ml/10fl oz white wine

Makes about 1.2 litres/2 pints

Put all the chopped vegetables into a large pan and cover with water. Add the garlic, peppercorns, coriander seeds, star anise and bay leaf and bring to the boil, then reduce the heat and simmer, uncovered, for 8 minutes.

Add the herbs and simmer for a further 3 minutes, then add the wine and remove from the heat.

Cover the pan and allow to cool, then leave in a cool place for 48 hours to marinate. Once marinated, strain the stock through a fine sieve. It can be either used immediately, covered and chilled in the fridge for up to 3 days, or frozen for up to 3 months.

Fish cream

One of the cornerstones of fish cookery, this sauce has great flavour and texture suitable for a wide range of uses. Add herbs, caviar or tomato as appropriate for specific dishes. It will keep in the fridge for 3–4 days, but does not freeze.

25g/1oz unsalted butter

2 medium shallots, peeled and finely chopped

4 button mushrooms, finely chopped

100ml/3½fl oz dry white wine

100ml/3½fl oz Basic Fish Stock (see page 181)

100ml/3½fl oz double cream

freshly squeezed lemon juice, to taste

sea salt and freshly ground black pepper

Makes 150ml/5fl oz

Melt the butter in a medium saucepan, add the shallots and mushrooms and cook over a low to medium heat, stirring occasionally, until softening but not colouring – 6–8 minutes.

Add the wine, bring to the boil and boil hard until almost disappeared. Quickly pour in the fish stock and again reduce until there is just a shiny glaze covering the bottom of the pan.

Stir in the cream and bring to the boil, then remove from the heat, taste and season with salt, pepper and lemon juice. Strain into a clean pan and reheat to serve.

tip

Fill ice cube trays with reduced fish stock (see page 181) and freeze to keep handy for making this sauce in a jiffy.

Butter sauce (beurre blanc)

Another cornerstone of classical French cooking, a good butter sauce partners just about any fish, adding richness and acidity in equal measure. Once made, it can be kept warm for up to 4 hours in a vacuum flask rinsed out with boiling water.

25g/1oz shallots, peeled and very finely chopped

2 tablespoons white wine vinegar

3 tablespoons dry white wine

2 tablespoons water

1 tablespoon double cream

125g/4oz unsalted butter, diced

freshly squeezed lemon juice, to taste

sea salt and cayenne pepper

Serves 4–6

Place the shallots, vinegar, wine and water in a heavy-based pan, bring to the boil and reduce over a high heat until just over a quarter remains. Add the cream and boil for 1 minute.

Now dump in all the butter and whisk for all you're worth, keeping the pan over the heat until you see any sign of the sauce boiling at the edges (conspicuous puffs of steam are a sure indication that the mix is too hot). If this happens, then remove it from the heat, but keep whisking. The target temperature for the mix is 50°C/120°F. If the temperature becomes too high, the sauce will boil and split, too low and the butterfat will start to set and also split. So try and keep it in the 50°C zone – which should be comfortable enough for you to poke a finger into – and you are guaranteed a lovely silky sauce. Purists may want to sieve out the shallots, but I leave 'em in.

Season the sauce with lemon, salt and cayenne and keep warm ready for use, but do not boil.

Clarified butter

Clarified butter is obtained by heating normal butter gently until the fat separates from the whey. Simmer the butter, removing any scum that forms on the surface, until a clear fat layer is formed with the liquid below. Strain the butter through muslin carefully, keeping the milky whey behind in the pan. This will keep in the fridge for ages – just remember to cover it or keep it in a screw-topped jar.

tip

You can do this just as easily in the microwave.

Basic mayonnaise

Making mayonnaise with olive oil creates an overpowering flavour, so I like to use groundnut oil instead. This will keep for up to seven days in the fridge.

1 egg yolk
1–2 tablespoons freshly squeezed lemon juice
1 tablespoon Dijon mustard
a pinch of sea salt
300ml/10fl oz groundnut (peanut) oil
a few drops of Tabasco sauce (optional)

Makes 300ml/10fl oz

Put the egg yolk, lemon juice, mustard and salt into a small bowl and whisk together well. Now, very gradually, whisk in the oil with an electric hand whisk until the finished mixture is thick and silky smooth; you may need to add some warm water if the mayo gets too thick.

Whisk in the Tabasco (if using) and a little more lemon juice to taste if you wish. Cover with some clingfilm and chill until needed.

Variation

For lemon mayonnaise, add the zest of 1 lemon and a few more drops of lemon juice to the basic recipe.

tip

Some chefs like to add 1–2 teaspoons of gastric to this mix to lift the flavour. A gastric is a 50/50 mix of sugar and vinegar boiled down to a syrup.

Basic white sauce

I always use one-and-a-half times as much fat as flour for a roux. That way, the roux melts over the base of the pan, allowing you to fry the flour in the butter and cook out the starch. It also avoids the dreaded 'golf ball' of floury dough that produces über lumps as soon as you add liquid.

40g/1½oz unsalted butter
25g/1oz plain flour
600ml/1 pint full cream milk
sea salt and freshly ground black pepper

Makes about 600ml/1 pint

Melt the butter in a small heavy-based saucepan. Add the flour and, using a wooden spoon, stir over the heat for 2–3 minutes, until it turns a light sandy brown colour and smells biscuity. Leave on the heat and, using a wire whisk, whisk in the milk in 2 or 3 goes, whisking well after each addition until it thickens before adding the next splash. Make sure it is well blended. Bring to the boil, whisking as it thickens. Once boiling, remove from the heat and season to taste.

If keeping the sauce, cover the surface with clingfilm to prevent a skin forming.

My basic dipping sauce

I find myself becoming increasingly addicted to this blend of hot, sweet, salty and sour. I nearly always add chilli flakes and chopped garlic, but feel free to experiment with other flavours.

3 tablespoons freshly squeezed lime juice
3 tablespoons Thai fish sauce (nam pla)
3 tablespoons water
1 tablespoon palm sugar (or golden caster)

Makes about 150ml/5fl oz, serves 4–6

Whisk all the ingredients together until the sugar has dissolved. Store in a sealed jar in the fridge for up to 1 week.

Try adding other flavourings to ring the changes: finely chopped garlic, fresh root ginger or chilli, very finely chopped carrot or courgette, and, of course, chopped fresh coriander and/or mint.

Basic pasta dough

Fresh pasta dough has a softer texture than dried and works well with the more delicate fish, such as sole and plaice. Fresh pasta is also essential for making ravioli and tortellini. Making it is much easier than you might think, and the secret of success is in getting the dough to the correct texture prior to rolling. Achieve this by making it in a food processor and ensure that the dough forms a 'crumb' similar to breadcrumbs before kneading. Once kneaded, the dough should have a texture similar to Plasticine. Always store the uncooked dough wrapped in clingfilm to prevent it drying out and cracking.

200g/7oz Italian "00" pasta flour

2 eggs

Serves 4 as a starter

Place the flour in a food processor and start giving it a whizz round. Add the 2 eggs and keep whizzing until the mixture resembles fine breadcrumbs (it shouldn't be dusty, nor should it be a big, gooey ball). This should take 2–3 minutes, but if it doesn't look right you can regulate the texture by adding more flour or egg until it's spot on. Alternatively, roll your sleeves up and do it by hand!

Tip out the dough onto a work surface and form into a ball shape. Knead it briskly for one minute. Wrap in clingfilm and rest for one hour before using.

Now cut the dough into 2 pieces. For each piece, flatten with a rolling pin to 5mm (¼ inch) thickness.

With the pasta machine at its widest setting, pass the dough through the rollers. Repeat this process, folding over the dough after each pass until the pasta is silky smooth and shiny. Now reduce the settings one at a time until the desired thickness is reached.

At this point, you can run the pasta sheet through the cutters to give either spaghetti (with the finer cutter) or fettucine. Use the thinnest setting for lasagne, ravioli and tortellini.